MW00416599

THE MENTAL GAME OF WRITING

How to Overcome Obstacles, Stay Creative and Productive, and Free Your Mind for Success

THE MENTAL GAME OF WRITING

How to Overcome Obstacles, Stay Creative and Productive, and Free Your Mind for Success

James Scott Bell

Compendium Press

Compendium Press
P.O. Box 705
Woodland Hills, CA 91365

ISBN 10: 0-910355-33-9
ISBN 13: 978-0-910355-33-9

Table of Contents

Introduction

Our doubts are traitors
And make us lose the good we oft might win
By fearing to attempt.
– Shakespeare, *Measure for Measure*

When I was first learning to play golf, at the age of forty-one, I went through that stage all new golfers go through. I call it the Space Odyssey phase.

Remember in the Kubrick film when that grunting hominid first discovers he can break things with a bone? He goes wild! Things breaking all over the place! Then he throws the bone into the air with a tremendous howl!

Well, I got to the point where my young golf swing was just breaking things all over the place, especially grass and dandelions.

So one day I was on a very easy course, a nice looking piece of land in Los Angeles, and I took out my five iron and proceeded to shank another ball into the water.

With a tremendous howl I flung my golf club, with both hands mind you, as far into the air as I could.

It whirligigged toward the heavens. I watched it, as if it were flying in slow motion, until it came to rest in a large, leafy bosom of a eucalyptus tree.

And did not come down.

It's probably still there, providing a perch for a weary sparrow.

As for this weary golfer, I considered giving up the sport altogether. Who needed the anxiety?

But I had fallen in love. There was nothing to compare with the feeling of that one great strike, which happened about once every 500 swings. I wanted to play this game. I wanted it to be part of my life.

Desperate, I began searching for golf books that would show me exactly what to do with my hands, hips, arms, hands, feet.

But then I came across a book that told me to attend to what was in my head. It was *The Inner Game of Golf* by W. Timothy Gallwey. The book made an astonishing claim. You could actually lower your score significantly by mastering what goes on inside your noggin.

You could learn to relax, perform under pressure, and make a repeatable swing. You could learn to get out of your own way, so you're not over thinking everything you do. The game would be more fun and you'd be better at it, too.

I was ready for anything! So I spent several months working on my mental approach to golf. And you know what? I didn't throw any more clubs. That was a partial victory! But I also got better. A little, not a lot, but at least I was headed in the right direction.

I learned that when you play golf you're actually supposed to *play* golf. It's a game. You play it. You don't think it.

It's before and after a round that you do your thinking, your analysis, your practicing.

You use what's called muscle memory to instill mechanics, and then when you get out on the course you just try to enjoy it. Sure, during a round you might correct something, or notice a hitch in your swing. (By the way, it's a lot better for you to notice it than for your playing partner to notice it, for there is nothing more annoying than having your partner telling you how to line up your shot as you are actually ... lining up your shot! It would be just as annoying to have your critique partner looking at your words as you're typing them and telling you not to do this and not to do that. *You just jumped out of her Point of View! Retype it!)*

When you write, you should write. You should play. Then you balance that with analysis and learning and training and drills.

You learn to get out of your own way.

For the writer, that means learning how to silence your inner critic. That's the part of your brain that has been trained since you began school—getting tested, getting teased because your blocks weren't lined up the right way according to the smarty-pants in your kindergarten class. Years and years of this have built up an inner critic the size of Godzilla.

The biggest part of the mental game of writing is learning ways to cut this monster down to size.

And then freeing yourself to write, learn, grow, handle rejection, keep going.

Rinse.

Repeat.

Do this, and you will begin to feel unstoppable.

And feeling it, you'll be it.

I've written this book because I believe the mental game of writing is as important as learning the craft. For it does not matter how much you know if you can't get yourself motivated to apply it. Especially when the proverbial chips are down.

After nearly a quarter century of making my living as a writer, I've gone through every iteration of the mental game of writing. And just as I learned to play an enjoyable round of golf, I learned how to keep writing with joy, too. Not that it always is, because there are challenges to overcome, most certainly.

But knowing in your head that you can overcome is a confidence builder like no other.

And when you're confident, you write better.

So let's build.

Decision

If you want to be a writer, you have to *decide* to be a writer.

There's a world of difference between wanting and deciding.

You can want to be a writer and sit around with mental images of yourself, daydreaming about having a line of readers waiting for you to sign copies.

Or you can decide to be a writer and wake up early each morning and type.

The first thing I did when I decided to be a writer—after ten years of believing I didn't have what it takes because that's what people told me, you're either born a writer or you're not—was go to Samuel French, a writer's store in Los Angeles, where I bought a black coffee mug with the word WRITER in gold on it.

It was for me, and me alone, to look at each day—and then prove it to myself by writing a quota of words.

I was a writer, because I decided to be.

Note, it was a long time before I told *anyone else* I was a writer. In my mind, I couldn't say that until the majority of my income was coming from the written word. (But that's just me. If you want to call yourself a writer in public, you go right ahead. And if someone scoffs or gives you a pitiful smile, make that person an ax murderer in your next book.)

The next thing I did was put inspiration in my office.

One of them was a two-page, full-color ad from a magazine. The ad was for the Apple Macintosh, early version. In this ad a guy is in his urban apartment, a nice view of the city outside the window, feet propped on the desk, petting a cat on his lap, and looking at his Mac.

He was dressed in jeans and a sweater.

The whole vibe was of a guy who worked for himself, at home, because the Mac let him.

I was a Mac guy myself, from the get-go, from the 1984 Super Bowl ad.

I saved that ad (I still have it) and looked at it frequently.

Then I found a postcard with one of my favorite writers, Stephen King, sitting in his workspace at home, his feet up on the desk, his dog right below him, word processor nearby. I framed it.

Then I found a photograph of John D. MacDonald, seated in his home office, pipe in mouth, fingers poised over the keys of his electric typewriter.

I framed that, too.

Finally, I was inspired by the career of Evan Hunter, who also wrote under the name Ed McBain. Prolific. Solid. Professional. I bought a hardcover of one of the Hunter titles, *The Moment She Was Gone*, and on the back was an author photo of Hunter, arms crossed, glaring. To me, a fellow writer, he seemed to be saying, "Write, damn you!"

So I put that book on one of my shelves, with the author photo facing out. Here's what I would see each day:

Silly?

Call it that if you like, but I remember being pumped up to write many, many times by looking at these icons.

And I've had a long and fruitful professional career that's still going.

And it will keep on going until I die.

Why?

Because I have decided it shall be so.
Have you decided to become a writer? To *stay* a writer?
Can you say it out loud to yourself?
Say it.
No one can silence you on that particular item.
You are a writer when you decide to be a writer.
Welcome to the fellowship.

Type

What type of writer have you decided to be?

For decades there has been a somewhat ambiguous distinction between the "serious" or "literary" writer, and the "popular" or "commercial" scribe.

In crass terms, the difference has sometimes been put this way: serious writers care about critics; popular writers care about dough.

It's not an issue of recent vintage. It was the premise of a 1943 Bette Davis film called *Old Acquaintance*. In this movie, Davis plays a serious author who is lauded by critics, but whose books don't sell. Her lifelong friend, played by Miriam Hopkins, cranks out a romance novel every year, and has become wealthy.

The point is, there has been a difference and a debate throughout the years. One of the most successful popular writers of all time, Mickey Spillane (creator of the PI icon Mike Hammer), was constantly being run down by serious writers who did not sell. To which he said, "Those big-shot writers … could never dig the fact that there are more salted peanuts consumed than caviar."

A great deal of this was fueled by simple envy. Someone labors over a novel for years and it sells 3,000 copies. Another cranks out three books a year that all hit the *New York Times* bestseller list. For the hyper-serious writer, that can seriously mess with their head.

Sometimes, though, a so-called literary novel will become a huge hit. Oprah Winfrey used to make it so whenever she chose a title for her book club. Other times a title just catches on and the author becomes something of a celebrity, like Jonathan Franzen. This occurrence, however, is rare.

Whatever type of writer you aspire to be, there are two primary considerations to think about. First, the market, the place where books are sold. Second, the kind of stories you burn to write.

On the popular website Writer Unboxed (Nov. 17, 2015), Dave King (co-author of *Self-Editing for Fiction Writers*) recognized a reason to consider what is selling in the market:

> Of course, in some ways you can't help writing to market. The point of writing is to give readers something they'll want to read. This is especially true if you're writing in a particular genre. Readers of romance, science fiction, horror, fantasy all expect their novels to deliver certain tropes, and it's up to you to provide them. If you give your readers a mystery without a crime, detective, or denouement, then you really aren't giving them a mystery.

Yet King rightly notes that mere formula is not enough. Otherwise a story can become what he terms "hack" work. To avoid that:

> When you bring something original to the mix – an approach to your characters that stretches the boundaries of the genre, a plot that doesn't simply string together the usual twists – then you are more likely to reach across genre lines to a larger market.

However–

> Completely ignoring the market can be as dangerous as pandering to it. If you deliberately turn away from your readers to follow your own, eccentric vision, you might wind up with something no one else will understand — or think is worth the bother.

King's conclusion:

> I understand the temptation to focus on the market. If you're having a hard time breaking into print, the siren song of the hack – boil down readers' expectations to a formula, then never color outside the lines – can be hard to resist. But bending your story to the market's will is a shortcut that won't get you where you want to go. The best way to reach the market is to throw everything you've got into telling the story you want to tell.

My conclusion is as follows:

First, the pro writer always considers the market, because it's just another way to refer to *people who buy books*. If you don't want to reach people who buy books you can certainly write for fun or therapy or to keep your fingers limber. But I'm going to assume you do want readers to buy your stuff. If so, it's essential to find out what's being bought.

But then! *Marry those considerations to what you love to write.*

Figure out that area where love and commerce come together.

It's like this Venn diagram. The sweet spot for you is right in that middle.

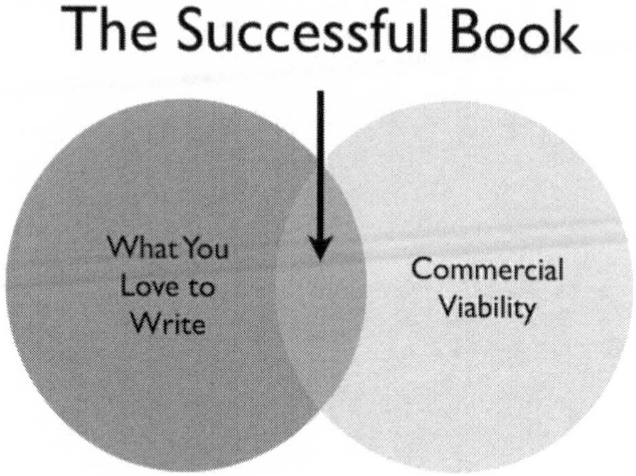

Definitely "tell the story you want to tell" but tell it with VOICE. As I argue in my book *VOICE: The Secret Power of Great Writing*, voice is what elevates and distinguishes one novel from another, and turns readers into fans.

So it's not a matter of what you love *versus* what will sell. It's a matter of finding that exquisite intersection where you're happy to park yourself and hammer out stories readers are actually going to buy.

Of course, selling (or selling a lot) may not be your goal. Maybe you're more interested in absolute, insular creativity, and damn the commercial torpedoes.

Great! You can write *despite* the market. You can decide to take that risk (unlike most risk-averse publishers these days). And every once in awhile such a book breaks out into huge and stunning success. Maybe 1% of the time. If you don't mind those odds, go for it.

(One nice thing about self-publishing is that you can experiment with short-form work, and see what takes wing.)

But there are many writers, as in the old pulp days, who are doing this to put food on the table and kids through college. They write for a market *and* they figure out how to love what they write.

What type of writer do you want to be?

Think about it. Analyze it. Make your choice.

Then write the best books you can.

Success

How do you define success?

The legendary UCLA basketball coach, John Wooden, defined success as "peace of mind which is a direct result of self-satisfaction in knowing you did your best to become the best you are capable of becoming."

The strength of this definition is that it puts success within everyone's reach. You can't control all outcomes, like where your book lands on a sales list or what reviewers say about your books.

What you can do is those things you know you must in order to become a better and smarter writer.

A few other definitions of success:

Poet Maya Angelou: "Success is liking yourself, liking what you do, and liking how you do it."

Winston Churchill: "Success is going from failure to failure without losing enthusiasm."

R. F. Horton, as quoted in *Elbert Hubbard's Scrapbook:* "Success lies not in achieving what you aim at, but in aiming at what you ought to achieve, and pressing forward, sure of achievement here, or if not here, hereafter."

Zane Grey: "These are the tests of true greatness—to bear up under loss, to fight the bitterest of defeat and the weakness of grief, to be a victor over anger, to smile when tears are close, to resist disease and evil men and base instincts, to hate hate and to love love, to go on when it would seem good to die, to seek ever the glory and the dream, to look up with unquenchable faith to something ever more about to be. These things any man can do and so be great."

So what is your definition?

Start by completing this sentence: *I want to be a writer because* _______________.

Now turn that into a success definition that puts you in control of the steps you can take.

For example, let's say you wrote this: *I want to be a writer because I love to express myself, and I hope to make some good money doing that.*

What might your success definition look like?

Success is finding joy in my writing, getting better at it, and producing books on a regular basis.

Take some time with this. Write out your definition of success, and review it from time to time.

Then determine what steps you need to take in order to make success a reality.

Which brings us to the subject of goals.

Goals

Why set goals? Because you can either control your own destiny or hand it over to circumstance. I'd much rather act than react. I'd rather have a plan than have time and tide devour me.

So now you should have three areas of life you're dreaming about: work, relationships and self (personal growth). Come up with three goals for each area.

Here's how:

a. Decide exactly what you want to accomplish

You must be specific here, and the goal must be something *you can make happen.*

For example, your goal cannot be to become a #1 *New York Times* bestselling author. Why? Because that's out of your control. You can't force bookstores and readers to buy your book.

What can you do instead? You can do what it takes to become a better writer. You can commit to studying the craft of writing and attending one writers' conference a year. You can commit to studying the market and learning what sells. *Those* are things you can control.

If your dream is to win a golf tournament, you set practice goals. That's what you have within your power.

If you want a certain income, you have to figure out what you can offer that is of value, and then work on that thing. A lawyer, for example, might decide to specialize in an area of law. He can then take courses and study that area thoroughly. He can set up meetings with mentors. He can do things that are within his power.

The results take care of themselves.

Go ahead now: write out specific goals, things you can actually control, and choose a top goal for each area of your life. You don't have to toss the other ones out. You can have a number of goals, whatever you like.

b. Record your goals

Recording your goals means write them down on paper or type them into a computer file. I actually like doing both. The act of writing down a goal, placing it on a card I can look at regularly, is a sensory way of getting that goal firmly implanted in my mind.

I have a corkboard program on my computer. On this board I have 18 index cards with my writing projects on them. These projects are in various stages, but I can see them every day.

I have another place for my get-off-my-butt goals. And still another document has my long-term goals for other parts of my life.

You can re-write these periodically, too.

Again, prioritize. This way you're going to be able to concentrate on the goals most important to you at any given time of your life.

c. Make plans for your goals

A plan is going to include two things: a deadline and a process.

Deadlines are important because a little time pressure keeps you moving forward. Write down the date you want to see your goal accomplished.

Next, write out a plan of action. What steps are you going to take to realize your goal?

For instance, if my goal is to finish a novel by December 31, I can figure out how many words I'll have to write between now and then. I divide that number by the number of weeks until the deadline. That gives me a weekly quota of words to shoot for.

Also, there might be research time I'll need to include. Maybe I have to go to the location I'm writing about and take some notes and photos. That would be included in the plan.

Just think of all the necessary steps and write them down. Then you can look at exactly where you are and what you need to do next. Check off the steps as you accomplish them. Do this for every goal on your list.

EXAMPLE:

Finish my novel, *The Sound of the Basketballs,* by December 31.

Need to write 6200 words per week.
Research trip to downtown library, micro-film.
Re-read Sherlock Holmes stories.
Take one full week at beach house.
Find someone who owns beach house.
Schedule freelance editor.

d. Take action every day

Do something, anything, toward your goals, every day. Sure, you're going to have days when things don't go right. But even on days where activity is limited you can find one thing that will be a step forward.

For example, I'm always prepared to "write" when I'm not writing. I have note paper with me and I can jot random thoughts as they occur. I try to keep my "boys in the basement" (the subconscious mind as described by Stephen King) busy in their work.

And when you do, you begin to feel enormous confidence. That, in turn, will motivate you to more action.

You'll be a perpetual goal-achieving machine.

e. Study, lean and grow in your goal areas

The best way to predict the future is to create it. You do that by study.

It's been a practice of mine from the beginning to set aside at least one hour a week for reading and studying in a particular area. I try to do more, but this is my minimum.

As a writer, I continue to read books on the craft. Even though I've written several of these myself and teach writing all over the country, my philosophy is if I can learn just one thing—or get a slightly fresh take on something I already know—it's worth it to me.

I buy books and read *Writer's Digest* magazine (where I was the fiction columnist for several years).

We expect brain surgeons to keep up on the medical journals. Why should it be any different for you (aside from the fact that when you make a mistake no one dies)?

Readers

When my daughter turned eight my wife and I decided to throw her a major birthday party. There was a video/laserdisc store near our home that had a small theater in the back. You could rent that place out for parties and the like. So that's what we did. We invited five or six of my daughter's best friends, ordered pizza and candy and popcorn and a cake. Our daughter was excited about the party of the year.

But what movie to show? My wife and I discussed this, and I practically insisted we show the Carroll Ballard film, *The Black Stallion.* I mean, come on. It had horses! Little girls love horses!

The party began.

Before the main feature, the proprietor of the store played a music video hawking the film *The Addams Family.* It featured MC Hammer before he was simply Hammer, and it was a hit. The girls stood up and danced around and laughed.

I sat back with a satisfied smile on my face. Champion Dad, that was me.

And then came *The Black Stallion.* It's truly one of my

favorite movies of that era. Magnificently shot, wonderfully acted.

But also lyrically deliberate (translation: leisurely. Slang: slow). And, as I soon found out, not the right movie for sugar-buzzed eight-year-old girls who had just been bouncing up and down to the moves and music of MC Hammer.

It was only about twenty minutes into the film when the first stirrings of boredom began to vibrate. Girls started chatting with each other. Some went to the bathroom and took their sweet time coming back. My daughter's eyes pleaded with me to do something.

Eventually I stopped the film and we got the owner to put on some cartoons. Then we moved on to cake and presents. Party saved!

But what had gone wrong? Something very simple. I had chosen a film that delighted *me*, that I thought everybody should like, especially a group of girls. But it was not a movie that delighted *them*. It was the wrong movie for the age group and occasion, which was a raucous get-together to celebrate a birthday and make some noise. They wanted to have fun and laugh.

In short, I failed to appreciate the needs of the audience.

Which is a mistake we dare not commit as writers. May I suggest the following principles be put in your mental lock box?

1. Your value as a professional writer is directly proportional to your value to readers

If you want to write what you want to write and don't particularly care who reads you, that's fine. You can be the local Starbucks laptop jockey. But if you are in this to be a pro, you must give thought to your readers. What are they looking for? Well ...

2. The overwhelming majority of readers want to be lost in a story in a dreamlike way

Which means you have to know how to weave those dreams. To do justice to readers means you take the time to figure out what they love and how to deliver it. You realize that all of us are wired to receive a story that has structure, involves characters we bond with, and creates unconscious delight in how it is told. That doesn't happen by accident.

3. You can challenge your readers, but don't expect them to embrace your challenge

It's fine to write material that requires readers to expend mental effort. Art can be many things, and challenging is one of them. Just know that you can't force readers to recognize your genius. And have the courage to ask yourself if you've crossed the border separating true artistic enterprise from self-indulgence.

4. Don't fall in love with your sentences

Beautiful words count for very little if there's no story, no characters worth caring about, no real plot. There's an old adage for writers that goes, "Kill your darlings." Stephen King likes to quote it, and it's attributed to a number of writers, like Faulkner and Oscar Wilde. But apparently it comes from a lecture on writing style delivered by Sir Arthur Quiller-Couch back in 1914. He was warning against "extraneous ornament" when he said:

> If you here require a practical rule of me, I will present you with this: 'Whenever you feel an impulse to perpetrate a piece of exceptionally fine writing, obey it—whole-heartedly—and delete it

before sending your manuscript to press. Murder your darlings.

Throw a party for your readers and don't force them to sift through what you think they ought to like. You win at the writing game when you determine to delight them.

Courage

Some time ago I was at a park near my home, sitting in a folding chair, soaking up some rays and fresh air. Mellowing out, as we say here in Los Angeles (when we are not driving, of course, for then it is war).

About a hundred yards away I saw a young man attaching a black rope around a tree. He tied the other end to another tree, so the rope spanned about twenty yards. Then he stepped on the rope and started walking.

Arms akimbo, he made it about half way before things started wiggling too much, and he jumped off.

He went back and tried it again.

And again.

There, in front of God and man and the squirrels, he was walking a tightrope.

It takes guts to do that. People walking by, watching, wondering if you'll fall. Maybe even hoping you will.

Then I thought about those guys who walk the tightrope in a circus. Or over Niagara Falls. I'm talking *real* guts there.

Why do they do it?

Because they want to. Maybe need to. It's what consumes their hearts.

Writers, it seems to me, are like tightrope walkers. It takes courage to put yourself out there, especially at the beginning, arms akimbo, people expecting you to fall. Maybe wanting you to.

And you do.

There are stumbles. Lots of them.

There is rejection.

There are pages of prose that stink.

There are family members that smirk.

And always lurking is the fear that you're not good enough, that you'll never make it, that it's all been a giant waste of time.

The question then is, what are you going to do about the fear?

1. Identify what you're afraid of

Name your fears. Put them down on paper (yes, paper, as we will use it later).

Some of the common fears about writing are these:

Do I have what it takes?
Will my mother approve?
Will I ever sell anything?
Will people think I suck?
What if I get bad reviews?
What if I never get an agent?

Write your list.

Then set it aside.

2. Know you're not alone

Dick Simon, one of the founders of Simon & Schuster, once said, "All writers without exception are scared to death. Some simply hide it better than others."

When I was just coming up in the fiction racket I heard an old pro I admired, who had a string of bestsellers, admit she was more scared now than ever when she sat down to work on a new book.

How could that be?

I determined that her fear was of not living up to the higher standards she now had. The more you write professionally, the more you come to know what your own weaknesses are, and how high a bar you keep setting for yourself.

My fear at the time was wondering if I'd ever get published, or once published, if I'd stay that way.

All over the map, writers have varying degrees of fear or, at least, anxiety.

You are not alone in this.

The only question is what do you do about it?

3. Channel your anxiety

"Fear is never enjoyable," writes Ralph Keyes in *The Courage to Write*. "But nerves are part of the writing process, even an essential part. That's what most working writers eventually come to accept. Anxiety is always here; a daffy old uncle in the attic who stomps about, rattles his chains, and makes a ruckus."

Keyes also points to the benefits of a little anxiety: it makes us more alert, more observant. The trick is to keep it from becoming debilitating.

You do that by channeling.

That simply means directing the negative energy into a positive direction.

Bruce Springsteen once said that it was actual desperation that led to artistic breakthrough.

> I've always believed the greatest rock and roll musicians are desperate men. You've got to have something bothering you all the time. My songs are good because … it's like in art and love, hey, one and one makes three. In music, if it makes two, you've failed, my friends. You know, if you're painting, if all you've got is your paint and your canvas, you've failed. If all you got is your notes, you've failed. You've got to find that third thing that you don't completely understand, but that is truly coming up from inside of you. And you can set it any place, you can choose any type of character, but if you don't reach down and touch that thing, then you're just not gonna have anything to say, and it's not gonna feel like it has life and breath in it, you're not gonna create something real, and it's not gonna feel authentic. So I worked hard on those things.

Remember that list you made earlier, on a piece of paper?

Take it to a fireplace, or some other safe repository of flaming material, light a match and burn the thing.

As it turns to ash, say, "I am done with you."

Then go write something you were afraid of writing before.

Creativity

"Think left and think right and think low and think high. Oh, the thinks you can think up if only you try."
– Dr. Seuss

Fiction writers create worlds and characters, and come up with plots and scenes and dialogue and descriptions.

Non-fiction writers create new ways of looking at things, and language and imagery to explain what they find. Narrative non-fiction writers use imagination to recreate history in fresh ways.

The ability to create, to imagine what hasn't been done before and render it in a pleasing fashion, is the very definition of the art of writing.

Some people are naturally more creative than others. Part of it may be brain wiring. Another part the way they were brought up and educated.

Did your teachers tell you never to color outside the lines?

Were you put down because you were a "dreamer"?

Were you frightened into being risk averse?

No matter, anyone can learn to be more creative. And here is how. The steps to creativity are as follows:

1. Prod your brain
2. Get lots of ideas
3. Do not censor anything
4. Rest
5. Assess

Let's have a look at each step.

Prod

Getting your imagination to come up with ideas is a matter of both intentional and subconscious stimulation. You can control the former with various exercises. The latter responds to the same stimuli, but also incorporates a huge network of neurons we never notice.

According to a 2013 article in *Popular Science* ("How Imagination Works"), cognitive scientists "hypothesize that our ability to imagine, to come up with mental images and creative new ideas, is the result of something called a 'mental workplace,' a neural network that likely coordinates activity across multiple regions of the brain."

Neuroscientists had long believed that exercising the imagination was largely a function of the visual cortex, that part of the brain that works with imagery. But a study at Dartmouth saw many other regions of the brain getting into the act when subjects were asked to be creative.

Which means this for the writer: you can choose from an infinite storehouse of possibilities when getting into the creative mode. Here are two methods I use often:

The Dictionary Game

Open a dictionary at random (I carry a pocket dictionary with me).

Find the first noun you see.

Write for five minutes about that noun, without stopping. The trick is to let your writer's mind take you wherever you want to go. Don't worry about making sense. Just write.

When you're done, look at the words and underline anything surprising or interesting to you.

Now write for five minutes on that.

You're panning for gold.

Ask what that material can mean to your work-in-progress. How can you apply it? Can you take some of the feelings and put them in a character? Does any of it suggest a plot twist?

You will *always* find something useful through this game.

The "What if?" Game

Start asking *What if?* about everything you see. Every day.

Driving, you spot a guy walking along the sidewalk pushing a shopping cart. Ask: "What if he was the son of a hitman, hiding out from his own family?"

Or: "What if he has just lost the love of his life?"

If you see a billboard with people on it, ask alternative questions about them. If it's an insurance ad featuring a family, ask: "What if that father has a secret he doesn't want his wife to know?"

Or you're sitting in Starbucks. You see a parade of people come through the door. Give each on a short "What if?"

What if that woman used to be a famous supermodel?

What if that man just killed a drug dealer?

What if that high school girl didn't make the cheerleader squad?

What if that boy just stole a bicycle?

Do this often and your mind will start working like this pretty much on its own.

And that's a good thing.

Get lots of ideas

This is really the key to creativity. Our minds usually jump to the familiar the first time we start creating. What you want to do is push yourself beyond the immediate, and drill down into the surprising.

When you are in a creative phase, make it a habit to create a list of your ideas. Give yourself a ten-idea minimum.

For example, you're going to write a car chase scene in an urban setting. You want something unique to happen during the chase.

Your mind might come up with the usual stuff you've seen in movies:

A fruit stand
A child crossing the street
A woman screaming
A baby carriage

Go beyond all that!

A chunk of freeway that falls
A mother duck and her chicks
A mime on a unicycle

Ducks? Really?

Really.

Some incredibly important research was done in this area. I want to give you the important clip from *The Harvard Business Review* (Dec. 1, 2015):

> What determines whether the ideas we generate are truly creative? Recent research of ours finds that one common factor often gets in

the way: we tend to undervalue the benefits of persistence.

In a series of experiments we observed that people consistently underestimated the number of ideas they could generate while solving a creative challenge. In one, we brought 24 university students into the laboratory during the week leading up to Thanksgiving and asked them to spend ten minutes coming up with as many ideas of dishes to serve at Thanksgiving dinner as they could. Then we had them predict how many more ideas they could generate if they persisted on the task for an additional ten minutes. After that, they actually persisted for ten minutes.

On average, the students predicted they would be able to generate around 10 new ideas if they persisted. But we found that they were actually able to generate around 15 new ideas.

Several similar follow-up studies we conducted produced the same result. We asked professional comedians to generate punch lines for a sketch comedy scene; adults to generate advertisement slogans for a product; and people to come up with tactics a charity organization could use to increase donations. In each of these experiments, participants significantly underestimated how many ideas they could generate while persisting with the challenge.

Importantly, after each study we asked a separate group of people to rate the creativity of the participants' ideas. Across the majority of our studies we found that ideas generated while persisting were, on average, rated to be more creative than ideas generated initially. Not only did participants

> underestimate their ability to generate ideas while persisting, they underestimated their ability to generate their most creative ideas.
>
> Why do we underestimate the benefits of persistence? It's because creative challenges feel difficult. People often have the experience of feeling "stuck," being unsure of how to find a solution, or hitting a wall with one idea and having to start over again. … [C]reative ideas take time. They are often generated after an initial period of thinking deeply about the problem, considering different ways to frame the problem, and exploring different possible solution paths.

The research is clear. Push yourself to come up with more ideas, past your comfort zone. And remember:

Do not censor anything

Learn to shut off your editorial mind when you make your creative lists! This is crucial, because what may seem silly to you is often the freshest idea (see above). And you'll only know that if you let the ideas flow and then move on to …

Rest

Give your subconscious mind a little space. Put the list away for a bit.

In the exercise above, after you've come up with ten or more ideas for your car chase scene, take a five or ten-minute break.

Lie down on the floor with your feet on a chair, so the blood rushes to your brain.

Or eat a Twinkie.

Anything non-writing related. Then …

Assess

Now, with fresh eyes, go over your list.

Draw a line through each idea that is *too familiar.*

Then look at what you have left and choose the idea that jumps off the page.

Exercise your creativity. Spend at least one half hour per week in pure creativity time. Come up with ideas, what ifs, titles, first lines. Play. Write in a journal. Let your mind run around.

One more thing: when you wake up in the morning, as soon as you can, write for three minutes, dumping whatever is in your waking-up brain onto a page. There is gold in that there head.

Discipline

In 1936, an American athlete shamed Hitler and his whole view of superiority. Jesse Owens, an African American, won four gold medals, proving his own superiority in the world of track and field.

That victory did not come easily. As Owens later put it, "We all have dreams. But in order to make dreams come into reality, it takes an awful lot of determination, dedication, self-discipline, and effort."

Writers have dreams. That's how we all start out. We dream of seeing our book on a shelf, or on countless e-readers.

But dreams are only vapor. They're made up of the same stuff as soap bubbles.

Unless you put legs on your dreams, you're just dwelling in a movie theatre in your mind, showing you great trailers.

Dreams can be motivators, they can be the start of a journey. But the journey upward is not easy.

Nor would you want it to be.

The enjoyment of success only happens when you feel you have, in some sense, earned it.

In *The Power of Negative Thinking,* Hall of Fame basketball coach Bobby Knight defines discipline this way: Discipline is recognizing what has to be done, doing it as well as you can do it, and doing it that way all the time.

He has another maxim: Having the will to win is not enough. Everyone has that. What matters is having the will to prepare to win.

Do, or do not. There is no try.

The Quota

You want to talk about discipline? I'll tell you about discipline. Anthony Trollope, that's what I will tell you about discipline.

Back in the days when you had to write your books with an actual pen or pencil, Anthony Trollope worked as a civil servant in England. Despite having a full-time job he managed to write over 40 novels. The way he did it is described in his autobiography. He set himself a quota of words and wrote to that quota every single day. He did his words before he got to work, or sometimes on the train. He wrote down the number of words he wrote every day in a log book. If he got to the end of a novel and still hadn't fulfilled his quota, he would take out a fresh sheet of paper and write *Chapter 1,* and begin a new novel.

Some people, mostly nose-in-the-air critics, read that and thought it was abysmal. Why, Anthony Trollope was nothing more than a writing machine!

I think Trollope would've considered that a compliment. But he was not merely a machine, he was a producer who felt and thought and had empathy for his characters.

In other words, he was a master novelist who disciplined himself to get the work done, daily.

Just like a guy with any other job.

I just don't understand people who think being prolific

means being less than stellar. In fact, I have found that when I am writing toward a "stretch quota" (a little more than I can comfortably do) I'm actually energized and my imagination gets to working in overdrive.

Try this:

First, figure out how many words a week you can *comfortably* write per week. Test this. Look at your normal weekly schedule and figure out your writing appointments. Keep these as if you were dealing with an employer (because you are: you). Write at a pace that is easy for you, and produce words at each session.

Next, add up a week's worth of work.

That's your starting number.

Up that number by 10%. This is your new weekly target. You want to have a word goal that is just a touch beyond your comfort zone.

Divide that number of words by six.

This number becomes your daily writing goal. Why six? Because I advocate taking one day off per week from writing, as it recharges my batteries. (Yes, I sometimes cheat, but don't tell anyone. Most of the time I take Sunday off, and am raring to go again on Monday.)

So let's say you are able to write around 4,500 words in a week without too much strain. Your weekly quota will be 4,950. That works out to 850 words a day, six days a week.

The nice thing about having a weekly goal is that you can account for days when you are not productive. Life intrudes. Stuff happens. Just do a little more on the other days to make up for the shortfall.

Also, if you are able to produce above your quota on a given day, that will take the pressure off other days.

Keep track of all the words you write on a spreadsheet. Have the spreadsheet total your daily and weekly totals.

How do you know how many words you've written on a project?

One way is via Scrivener. This tremendous writing program is what I use for all my projects now. It has a target function, which enables you to see how many words you write during any given session. You can choose your own targets. It also shows you the cumulative total of your output.

If I'm writing a project in Word, I first record the word count. Then after my session I simply subtract that number from the new count. Or I'll highlight the new words I've written, and Word tells me how many words are in that "chunk."

If you don't make your quota one week, forget about it. Just start fresh the next week. The main thing is to keep a record and hold yourself accountable for hitting your number. If you put that number in your mind, and tell yourself you are going to reach it even if you have to forgo some other things, like watching Monday Night Football, do it. The more you train yourself to meet your quota, the more you will feel the power of momentum.

Playfulness Still Lives

There is a big part of the creative process that involves *not* thinking, just going for it. Ray Bradbury said he would wake up every morning and step on a "land mine," that land mine being himself. Only later would he begin to assemble the pieces. He would play, he would allow whatever was in his mind to pour out onto a page. Then he would look for the order.

Now that's a fun thing to do as a writer, but it is not the only thing. Every now and again I run across a teacher claiming this is the *only* way to write. If taken to heart, it will only lead to frustration for the writer. Because at some point in the writing process you are going to have to arrange things for the most important person of all—the reader.

They don't care how much you play. They care about what they can understand and relate to.

You can't play all the time. Even children have to be talked into cleaning up their rooms.

One of the secrets of the mental game of writing is learning when to play and when to restore order. When to blow up whatever you have, start again, play some more, and put in some new order.

Stories without order are called experimental. They have a very limited reach. If you don't mind that, and if you get artistic satisfaction out of that kind of thing, by all means go for it. Just understand that your audience will be small. I suppose once-in-a-generation an experimental novel breaks through to a few thousand people, and perhaps gathers some awards. Maybe once every fifty years such a novel will be taught in college classrooms.

But most writers I know want to be able to share their writing with a fairly wide audience. That requires the discipline of storytelling.

Growth

Jack London, who was America's leading literary "rock star" at the start of the 20th Century, set himself a rigorous training program. In his largely autobiographical novel, *Martin Eden,* London describes what the young, driven, and self-educated Martin did to learn how to write:

> Reading the works of men who had arrived, he noted every result achieved by them, and worked out the tricks by which they had been achieved—the tricks of narrative, of exposition, of style, the points of view, the contrasts, the epigrams; and of all these he made lists for study. He did not ape. He sought principles. He drew up lists of effective and fetching mannerisms, till out of many such, culled from many writers, he was able to induce the general principle of mannerism, and, thus equipped, to cast about for new and original ones of his own, and to weigh and measure and

> appraise them properly. In similar manner he collected lists of strong phrases, the phrases of living language, phrases that bit like acid and scorched like flame, or that glowed and were mellow and luscious in the midst of the arid desert of common speech. He sought always for the principle that lay behind and beneath. He wanted to know how the thing was done; after that he could do it for himself. He was not content with the fair face of beauty. He dissected beauty in his crowded little bedroom laboratory … and, having dissected, and learned the anatomy of beauty, he was nearer being able to create beauty itself.

The French writer Voltaire believed that originality is "nothing but judicious imitation." He was, as he was wont to do, overstating the matter. But there is a small scrap of suggestion in that quote. Imitating judiciously can lead to the building up of a more creative writing brain.

Think of it this way: you have, right now, a unique voice. One of the most important things you can do is learn how to let that voice out, without holding anything back.

But you can also expand your voice by imitating other voices you admire.

Many writers of the past used to copy, by hand, passages from authors they admired. The object was not to end up sounding like them, but to soak in the *sound of words.* Then, when you set out to write your own stories, you have increased, almost exponentially, your stylistic possibilities.

Of course, you do a little of this every time you read a writer you admire and linger over the language.

Just take that a step further.

Select a few authors whose style moves you. Gather their books around, or call them up on your e-reader.

Find pages you particularly like.

Read the page once silently.

Then read it again, out loud.

Next, copy the page word for word, *by hand*. There is added stimulus to the brain when you write with a pen on paper.

Finally, read the copied page once through.

And that's it.

Do a page like this once a week for a year. You will be amazed at how much better you write at the end of that term.

Self-Study

There are 7 Critical Success Factors (CSFs) in fiction: plot, structure, characters, scenes, dialogue, voice, meaning (or theme).

To the extent that you improve one of these areas, your writing grows stronger.

If you improve in all of them, your writing blasts up several levels.

To grow, you can break down each area and design a self-study program.

That's what I did early in my career. I'd figured out plotting, and turned in a novel that was part of a new publishing contract. The superb editor identified a weakness in characterization.

Which ticked me off.

But also made me do something about it.

I bought a couple of good books on the subject of creating characters, pulled out articles I'd saved from *Writer's Digest*, and selected half a dozen novels I'd read where the characters were particularly strong.

For weeks I studied the material, took notes, and applied them to my manuscript.

The book I finally turned in became a bestseller, and took me to another level.

I've been a self-study student ever since.

Get started on your own course by assessing, as objectively as possible, your competency in the 7 CSFs of Fiction. Get outside help if you need it, from friends or crit partners. Put feelings aside. Total honesty is called for.

On a scale of 1-10, 10 being perfect (and an impossible score), how do you rate?

Plot	____
Structure	____
Characters	____
Scenes	____
Dialogue	____
Voice	____
Meaning	____

Now, arrange these areas in order, from the weakest to the strongest.

Start by designing a six-week self-study program for your weakest area, then move on to the next. (In the last chapter of this book, *Further Resources*, you'll find a list of my books by topic area.)

Production

"The most critical thing a writer does is produce."
— Robert B. Parker

In 1907, Mr. Henry Ford declared he was going to make a motor car for the great multitude of Americans. He was not satisfied with the slow process of making one car at a time through laborious design.

Ford and his team of engineers came up with the car known as the Model T. It was a no-nonsense, one-color auto. While this lowered the price of a car for many, it still was not a low enough price for most people in the country to afford.

So Henry Ford and his crack team developed the concept of the assembly line for the automobile.

And history was changed.

The Ford assembly line incorporated four principles: interchangeable parts, continuous flow, division of labor, and reducing wasted effort.

Which is exactly what the productive writers should emulate!

Interchangeable parts: This means that you can use all of your craft knowledge—no matter what kind of book, story, or genre. The more you work and study, the better you become at using these tools.

Continuous flow: By which I mean your best pal, quota. We have covered this subject under "Discipline."

Division of labor: The Most Interesting Man in the World (Dos Equis commercials, remember?) once talked about the secret of life. He said, "Find the thing that you don't do well, and then don't do that thing."

The same can be said for the writer. What you should be concentrating on is writing and getting better at your writing. When it comes time to publish, if you go the traditional route, you need an agent. The agent will handle the finding a publisher part.

If you are going to self-publish, you need to know how to assemble a team for each book. You'll need beta readers, a good editor, a proofreader, a cover designer. You would be foolish to try to do all of these things yourself.

Reducing wasted effort: When you write, write with a purpose. You can even write randomly if your purpose is to exercise your writing brain, free yourself up. But the majority of your writing time should be on those projects which you hope to sell to a publisher or directly to readers.

And when you write, *write*. What do I mean? I mean do everything in your power not to be distracted by other things.

No email.

No internet.

No social media.

No phone calls.

Keep your mind on the page in front of you for as long as long as possible.

There's your assembly line.

Plan five and six projects ahead

Be like a movie studio. Have one greenlighted project going (what we call your work-in-progress, or WIP) and have two or three "in development" and two or three "optioned."

In development means you're doing some planning, some notes, some character backstory work, some plotting. If you're a pure pantser, at least take some random notes about the plot and keep them in a file or notebook. If you're wise, you'll develop your idea into an elevator pitch that will make a reader lust after your book. That's right, lust.

Work on that pitch until you're convinced it would pull a massive audience into a movie theater.

By *optioned* I mean having a simple What if premise that seems promising to you. I have a file with about 100 of these, and periodically I look them over and re-prioritize them. If one keeps sticking to the top of the heap, that's the one I will move into development.

You should always have a work in progress (WIP) and four other works in various stages of development. When you finish your WIP, take the most promising of your developed projects and put that on the front burner.

Which one is the most promising?

Remember our Venn diagram back in the chapter on the type of writer you want to be. Have yourself a studio meeting and figure out which one will be given the next green light.

Write even when you're not writing

Part of your mind is always at work on something creative. Your subconscious mind works without you knowing it. Your conscious mind can work, too, even when you're not at the keyboard.

Carry around a notebook, or use a smartphone app, to

take notes on the things you see, the sparks for ideas, and on things that occur to you about your WIP or developing projects.

Writer's Block

In *Fire Up Your Writing Brain* by Susan Reynolds (Writer's Digest Books), the author suggests five reasons a writer experiences block:

1. You've Lost Your Way
2. Your Passion Has Waned
3. Your Expectations Are Too High
4. You Are Burned Out
5. You're Too Distracted

I'd like to suggest another: fear of failure, and its cousin, fear of *finishing*. This happens when you're getting to the end of your novel, or are working on a subsequent draft. You find ways to keep from writing because you're afraid that once you finish the thing it won't be any good.

That leads to procrastination.

The only way to deal with procrastination is to wait it out.

Joking.

In dealing with blockage, I can't improve on what Nancy Hathaway had to say in an interview on advicetowriters.com:

> [If you have writer's block] force yourself to write non-stop for twenty or thirty minutes: no deletions, no erasures, no pauses. If that doesn't work, take a break. Take a walk. Pack up your writing supplies and go someplace new. Sit in a coffee shop, find a cozy spot in a library, go to a park. If you're truly desperate, go away for a few

days. Take a train to a distant city and write onboard (on Amtrak, you can actually plug in your computer. But coffee is essential: without it, the train will rock you to sleep.) It often helps to do something entirely nonverbal, like making a collage or playing music. And it always helps to understand that writer's block is a widespread malady. To strengthen your feeling of solidarity with the scribbling classes, watch these movies: *The Shining, Misery, Barton Fink, Deconstructing Harry,* all of which explore the consequences of writer's block.

Further Production Notes

Success expert Denis Waitley has the following suggestions for making hard work enjoyable (from his book *Flextactics):*

1. View the work you're engaged in as a *challenge.* If it's something you're used to, find ways to make it better or higher.

2. Approach what you're doing as if it is the first time you're doing it. Make it FRESH.

3. Follow the "as if" principle. When work is dull, make it a game, AS IF it was interesting. Find personal creativity in it.

4. Write down your accomplishments along the way to your goal.

5. Keep the end result in sight. Always see the BIG PICTURE and BENEFITS of the goal.

Uniqueness

"Build a better mousetrap, and the world will beat a path to your door." That old chestnut is usually attributed to Emerson, who may actually have put it this way:

"If a man can write a better book, preach a better sermon, or make a better mousetrap than his neighbor, you will find a broad hard-beaten road to his house."

Or his Amazon author page.

What we're talking about here is something entrepreneurial types like to call a Unique Selling Proposition, or USP.

The Unique Selling Proposition is *that factor or consideration presented by a seller as the reason their product or service is different from and better than that of the competition.*

With so many products out there in every category, consumers are looking for the best bang for their buck, and the best (e.g., most efficient, most convenient, most entertaining, etc.) product available.

Someone bringing a new product to market has to find a way to make it distinctive and better than other products in its category.

But if I go out and sell a mousetrap that's just like all the others, how can I expect to win over new customers?

Or readers, because they have an overwhelming amount of content to choose from. You as an author need to give them a reason to choose you.

Every author needs a personal Unique Writer Proposition—UWP.

Think of it this way. Say you love detective novels and your favorite writer is Michael Connelly. You don't really analyze why you dig Connelly, you just know that at the end of one of his books you've had an experience you want to repeat.

Now here comes Benny Wannabe, a new author, who is putting up his own detective novels for sale. When you read one, nothing about it really stands out. You finish it, and it's okay, but you are not left with the feeling you have when you read Connelly.

How likely are you to go seeking out Wannabe's other books?

(This is an appropriate moment to repeat another of my favorite quotes, from that hardboiled master Mickey Spillane: "The first chapter sells the book; the last chapter sells the next book." Connelly's last chapters do that for me.)

Thus, I propose that one of the first things you need to figure out as a writer is your UWP.

How do you find it?

First, look within to see what you already offer.

Next, add unique value.

Finally, strive to create books that deliver that value, every time.

1. Look Within

When I started out in traditional publishing, the big buzzword was *brand.* Every author had to have one, because that's how publishers sold you to bookstores, and bookstores to readers.

My brand at the beginning was as a lawyer writing legal thrillers. At a brainstorming session with some other writers, where we came up with taglines for our brand, I took the title of F. Lee Bailey's autobiography, *The Defense Never Rests,* and changed it to, *The Suspense Never Rests.*

A few years later I looked back on the books I'd authored and tried to detect a central theme. I found it. I determined that the main theme I write about is *justice.* The quest for it, the need for it, the fight for it. That hums throughout my novels. Having recognized that, I embraced it.

That was step one in finding my UWP.

2. Added Value

Now look at your work and ask yourself three questions:

a. What do I do well?
b. What can I do better?
c. What are my unique "add ons"?

I did this fifteen years ago. What I did well was plot (I had to learn how to do this at the start of my writing journey, and finally got it) and dialogue.

What I needed to do better was character and scenes. So I instituted a self-study program in both areas. (By the way, growing in the craft is on ongoing project. I'm always trying to find a way to do things better.)

Finally, what are some of the things I bring to my fiction that are particular to me? They turned out to be:

- A bit of humor mixed in with the suspense (a la my favorite director, Alfred Hitchcock).

- Spicy minor characters.

While other authors do these things as well, these areas filter through my unique personal makeup: humor shaped by a childhood bathed in *Mad* magazine, adolescence steeped in Woody Allen comedies, and college years watching the early seasons of SNL (still the best). These were also areas I was getting good feedback on from readers. I knew then that these were things I needed to keep emphasizing in my books.

3. Deliver the Goods

Once you have determined your own UWP (and it's good to write it down in 100 words or less, and tweak it from time to time), you have a model to shoot for. You write your book and revise the draft, keeping these things in mind. You get feedback from Beta readers and freelance editors.

And through it all, try to keep a picture in your mind of a tired mother or father, a busy professional, an overextended student. They have a small window of time for reading pleasure, and they've picked your book.

Remind yourself this time is sacred and you have been given the gift of trust.

Be unique. For them.

Joy

Zest. Gusto. How rarely one hears these words used. How rarely do we see people living, or for that matter, creating by them. Yet if I were asked to name the most important items in a writer's make-up, the things that shape his material and rush him along the road to where he wants to go, I could only warn him to look to his zest, see to his gusto." (Ray Bradbury, *Zen and the Art of Writing*)

Do you really want to write? Or do you just want to make money?

Listen: I have nothing against making money, so long as it is accomplished legally and morally (the two are not always the same). Have at it if you like, if you think you can do it by way of the written word. Thinking commercially and delivering a product is a fine way to make it, if you can.

Do you see that IF up there in the last sentence? Oh, what universes are held in that pair of letters! IF IF IF … the uncertain IF of the writing life!

But there's a way to stuff those letters with life, gusto, vitality, joy, aliveness!

And that is what I'm talking about here, in this part of the mental game of being a writer, a real writer who cares just as much about the words as about the money. Who in fact could not be satisfied with the latter if the former is not coming from his heart and soul.

"The first thing a writer should be," writes Bradbury, "is excited. He should be a thing of fevers and enthusiasm. Without such vigor, he might as well be out picking peaches or digging ditches; God knows it'd be better for his health."

Here's what you must do: Never write anything again, and I mean anything, until you feel the joy in it.

Even a grocery store list. Don't write anything on that list until you visualize the ice cream freezer, the display with the rib-eye steaks, the row upon row of cereal boxes, the eggs! Aren't eggs wonderful? They do so many things!

Now write that list.

And your next story, or blog post, or tweet, or novel, just pause for a second and feel it, wait for that inner electricity to snap in you, and write!

That goes for ideas, too.

I love to develop ideas.

I spend a portion of my week just making stuff up, randomly, first lines mostly. Here are two that I made up that I am burning to use, but haven't got around to yet (and may have by the time you read this, so don't even think about using them):

I was doing about eighty, with Samuel Cornell's left leg thumping around in my trunk, when I saw the cop car in my rear-view mirror.

I stood up in my bathtub, dripping and naked, and saw three Jehovah's Witnesses staring at me through the window.

I'm delighted I wrote these! I'm giddy about them. And even if I never attach a whole story to them, they have given me joy and zest, and those stay with you even when you write another project entirely.

Is it all unicorns and rainbows? Of course not! There are times when writing is like tearing flesh off a wounded wildebeest in a death-battle for survival. There are days you don't want to write another word, or see a book, or hear about anybody else writing anything.

Yes, there will be times when you don't feel the joy *on that particular day.*

But if you can still think of your project with confidence, you push through. The joy will return.

"A literary career should not be a career but a passion … A writer without passion is like a body without a soul. Or what would be even more grotesque, like a soul without a body."
- Edward Abbey

Habits

There are some people who like to exercise.

I am not one of them.

But I know I have to do it. In fact, I have to make it a habit.

Sometime ago I noticed how hard it was for me to work myself up into getting out on the treadmill early in the morning. Truth be told, there were many mornings I just said the heck with it, and promised myself I would work out later in the day. Which I almost never did.

This got me thinking about procrastination. Which I have been putting off.

Ahem.

One of the ways to defeat procrastination on a big project is to break it down into smaller bites, and then take that first bite. That first step. Not thinking about what comes next.

So I decided to try that with my exercise routine. Instead of thinking about getting out on the treadmill for half an hour, doing reps on my total gym, coming inside and taking a shower, I decided to try doing just one thing by 7 AM four times a week.

That thing was getting in my workout clothes.

Nothing else. I just set a goal to get in my exercise togs by 7.

That was easy to do.

Then I discovered it was much easier for me to step into the garage and fire up the treadmill.

It worked amazingly well. The small habit of getting dressed led to the larger habit of working out.

Getting in the writing habit can work the same way.

Here are a couple of suggestions.

First, think about allowing yourself to write something, anything, first thing in the morning. I've talked about the writing quota. I've used the trick I called the Nifty 350 for many years. That is, I try to get down 350 words before I do just about anything else.

For you it might just be 50 words. You can do that. Anybody who wants to be a writer can do that much. Try it, and I think you'll find yourself wanting to continue.

Second, you can do what Anne Lamott suggests in her terrific writing book, *Bird by Bird.* It's called the one-inch frame.

> [A]ll I have to do is to write down as much as I can see through a one-inch picture frame. This is all I have to bite off for the time being. All I am going to do right now, for example, is write that one paragraph that sets the story in my hometown, in the late fifties, when the trains were still running. I am going to paint a picture of it, in words, on my word processor. Or all I'm going to do is to describe the main character the very first time we meet her, when she first walks out the front door and onto the porch. I'm not even going to describe the expression on her face when she first notices the blind dog sitting behind the wheel of her car—just what

> I can see through the one-inch picture frame, just one paragraph describing this woman, in the town where I grew up, the first time we encounter her.

When I was a kid there was a famous novelty sign that started showing up on desks. It said, *Don't just do something, stand there.*

Ha ha. It was the reverse of the truism that you have do something, anything, to get anywhere.

You can have the novelty sign if you like. But don't do what it says.

Do one little thing toward your writing instead.

Validation

When self-publishing took off in 2008-09, and previously unknown authors started selling thousands of books via Amazon, the collective body of writers—published and unpublished—got hit with digital gold fever. It was like California in 1848, only this time Sutter's Mill was the Kindle store.

Many scribes sold their farms in Ohio and headed West to hit it big.

Some actually did.

Others went bust.

Still others just kept at it, kept working and growing as authors and entrepreneurs. More and more of these have managed to make a living as writers, or at least establish a steady monthly income stream.

During those early gold rush years I had many conversations with writers, at conferences and online. They all wanted to know if they should jump into the indie revolution with both feet or merely stick a toe in the water. The unpublished ones wondered if they should keep knocking on the doors of the Forbidden City (my term for the traditional publishing kingdom) or dive directly into self-publishing.

There were two reasons writers hesitated over the latter course.

First, there were dire warnings being issued by agents, editors and traditionally published writers that self-publishing would put a permanent taint on the writer, forever foreclosing any hope of breaking into the Forbidden City.

This warning had some merit. When self-publishing was print-based, very few writers ever managed to make a go of it, let alone produce a book that was lauded and in demand. Most of the time the books sucked. Which should not surprise us if we know Sturgeon's Law ("Ninety percent of everything is crap.")

The second big reason writers hesitated about going indie is exemplified by a conversation I had with a writer who had been rejected by agents for several years. It went something like this:

"How's the writing going?" I asked.

Sigh. "Hanging in there. Got three more rejections from agents."

"Have you tried submitting to a publisher directly?"

"Once. Never heard back."

"Have you thought about self-publishing?" (This was around 2011, when the self-publishing rush was hot. Barry Eisler had just walked away from a $500,000 traditional contract to strike out on his own.)

She shook her head. "I guess I really want the validation of being published by a New York house."

There it was. The V word.

Validation.

What exactly is it? And why do so many writers crave it?

The word *validation* means "to give official sanction, confirmation, or approval to." It's a stamp of status, granted to persons or documents by some outside authority.

For a writer, validation can come in many forms:

It is an agent saying yes to representing you.

It is a publishing house acquiring your manuscript.

It is being honored with an award from a recognized organization.

It is being included in conversations with successful writers, who acknowledge you and give you literal or virtual pats on the back.

It is seeing your name on the cover of a printed book the first time as you open the box sent by your publisher.

Or spotting your book on the shelf at Barnes & Noble.

That's validation, and there is nothing wrong with it. It feels good.

But that's where a writer can get trapped—in *feelings*. For validation can also be a siren. It's what Odysseus heard when lashed to the mast. It can take away your rational mind and drive you mad.

If you don't watch out, your desire for outside approval can become a requirement for your inner well-being.

Which is exactly what the Stoic philosophers warned about.

The way to unease in your soul is to worry about the things you cannot control. And validation is something that is out of your hands.

Marcus Aurelius observed: "Perhaps the desire of the thing called fame torments you. See how soon everything is forgotten, and look at the chaos of infinite time on each side of the present, and the emptiness of applause, and the changeableness and lack of judgment in those who pretend to give praise, and the narrow span of time it is given, and be quiet at last."

Do you really need validation from the outside to feel accomplished?

What will happen to you if you don't get it? Will you then consider yourself a failure?

Don't let outside forces control you!

And don't let the quest for validation take away from hard-headed assessment of your career.

If you desire the validation of a traditional book contract, concentrate on your writing, on becoming the kind of writer that a publishing company wants to publish.

Just don't let yourself be chained to the need for approval.

You don't need approval.

What you need is confidence in yourself, and a good work ethic.

Luck

On Joe Konrath's blog, September 17, 2015, the ever-understated opinionator wrote:

> Some people don't like me preaching on and on about how luck is possibly the single most important factor of success.
>
> Some of these folks insist that good writing will always find an audience.
>
> Some say those with success deserve it.
>
> Some say my insistence that luck is important is a form of humble bragging, since I've sold a few million books.
>
> Some don't like the fact that luck is beyond their control, and they believe talent and hard work always win out.
>
> Some think they make their own luck.
>
> I'll bite. Let's say I'm wrong. Let's say luck isn't as big of a factor as I think.
>
> Have you reached the level of success you

> want? If so, and you don't believe luck was involved, good for you. I suppose you can make a case for yourself, the same way every self-made millionaire makes a case when they write their inevitable "How I Did It" books. I don't know how many people have read the Essays of Warren Buffet and then became billionaires, but perhaps a lot have. Maybe good, solid advice, a strong work ethic, and loads of talent, coupled with a how-to template, can make anyone a raging success.
>
> But what if you aren't a raging success, and you still don't believe in luck?
>
> Well, maybe you suck.

Konrath is not playing self-esteem mommy here. He's more like R. Lee Ermey in *Full Metal Jacket.* "Maybe you're incapable of putting out good books," he says, "no matter how much time you spend at it."

Ouch.

What are you going to do with a line like that?

Just like the apple-cheeked marines under the unrelenting drill sergeant, you have two choices.

You can fold and quit.

Or you can get tough and keep going.

Choose get tough.

If you're a real writer, meaning someone who has to write, who desires to tell stories, who has an inner fire to put words down, you keep writing no matter what.

Which means you have to do something about your writing weaknesses.

But know this: All writers have weaknesses. It's just that some are more apparent than others.

I once heard a professional golfer talking about the difference between the pros and skilled amateurs. He said professionals simply don't make as many mistakes. Over time, their missed shots will be by smaller margins than the amateurs.

That's a good analogy for the difference between writers who sell and those who do not (or not as much they would like). Even A-list writers make mistakes. But there are fewer of them, and not many are egregious.

So be honest about your weaknesses. Find people who will tell you what you need to work on.

You can hire an editor, or go to something like the Writer's Digest 2nd Draft service.

You can find some readers who will give you honest feedback.

Once you identify weak points, do something to improve them.

Read craft books.

Attend a writers' conference and applicable workshops.

Write your quota and apply what you learn.

And while that still doesn't guarantee any specific level of success, it does improve your odds. Which is what "luck" is really all about.

When I was a young and impetuous college roustabout, my roomies and I would take occasional trips to Vegas. I learned the blackjack system in a famous book, Beat the Dealer. What that meant was I could get just about even with the house advantage. Which also meant, over time, I would do better than the hardware store owner from Tulsa who relied on pure luck when asking for a hit on a 10–7.

As you get better at the fundamentals of the craft, and as you produce more work, your odds will improve.

As one wag put it, "The harder I work, the luckier I get."

But what if luck doesn't happen the way you want it to?

I'll tell you: It does not matter in the slightest to a real writer!

A real writer never gives up, because that's the only sure way to lose.

Don't let luck or fate or fear stop you from doing what you should do every day of your life: write!

(Okay, not every day. You get a pass for funerals, family crises, arrests, car crashes, food poisoning, driving from L.A. to Colorado, and Disneyland. Other than that, you write).

You don't want to be sitting in a bar twenty years from now, hoisting your third brew, muttering to the stranger next to you, "Yeah, I used to be a writer. It's a tough racket."

You are a writer, so keep writing, keep growing, keep hammering away, and don't spend one minute grousing about luck.

Carpe Typem.

Seize the Keyboard.

Noise

Some writers like absolute quiet when they write.

Others like to have a little music going.

Still others like to write in public places, like coffee houses and delis.

What level is right for you?

A Little Ambient Noise, Please

Research into the area of creativity and "white noise" asserts that a moderate level of sound helps creative people in their work. What appears to happen is that more parts of the brain are pinged when there's a bit of background noise going on than when there is total silence. You are working consciously on one thing, with particular focus, while other parts of your brain below the conscious level are turning gears and yanking pulleys. And every now and then the foreman sends up an idea your consciousness grabs hold of.

Some of the popular sounds for this are:

Coffeehouse

I don't know what it is about this type of noise, but it seems to be quite effective for the writer. Maybe it's because there's language going on in the background, as well as the sound of dishes and the like. Perhaps that stimulates the language center of our own brain.

Personally, I like to work live in coffee joints. But if I don't go out, I can tune into Coffitivity.com. I set the level of the noise and off I go.

Since I use Scrivener for my writing, I utilize one of its features in concert with the coffee house sounds. Scrivener gives you the option of typing your page while setting a background view on your monitor. I use a photo of the interior of my favorite delicatessen, Langer's in Los Angeles. So it's like I'm there, writing.

The only problem with this is that after about two hours I find I'm dying for a hot pastrami on rye, with coleslaw.

Rain

The sound of rain is good for the stressed-out writer. It has a calming effect which removes obstacles in your mind, like worry or anger.

Sometimes you need that, and can find it in places like Rain.simplynoise.com.

Other noises

Maybe you'd like to try another type of noise, like wind or ocean or street. I find I love the steady beat of a train on a track. These and more are available at Defonic.com.

Experiment around. Try different combinations.

Go a little louder if you're writing action, and a little lower if you're in a quiet scene.

In fact, you can go a step further by choosing music to go with the mood you're trying to create.

Music for Mood

In an article in the online *Japan Times* (1/16/2016) titled "Murakami is right about jazz and the brain," the author touched on the effects of emotion on creativity.

> U.S. neuroscientists at Johns Hopkins School of Medicine in Baltimore, Maryland, scanned the brains of jazz pianists while the musicians were improvising songs on a small keyboard.
>
> The scientists found that brain circuits known to be involved in creativity changed their activity when different emotions are expressed. In other words, emotion — in this case, simply whether the musician was creating happy or sad music — caused different parts of the brain's "creativity network" to operate.
>
> "The bottom line is that emotion matters," says Charles Limb, a neuroscientist at the University of California, San Francisco. "It can't just be a binary situation in which your brain is one way when you're being creative and another way when you're not. Instead, there are greater and lesser degrees of creative states, and different versions. And emotion plays a crucially important role in these differences."

One way to stimulate the right mood for writing is by

using movie soundtracks. I like these because they don't distract me with lyrics. It's pure music piped directly into my brain.

I've created playlists for various moods: suspense, heartfelt, happy, distressed. Depending on what my Point of View character wants and the tone I desire, I start that playlist going and write. Often I'll combine the playlist with one of the other sounds mentioned above.

As writers, we want to give our brains every advantage in the act of creation. Don't lock it up in a silent room. Give it some noise!

Stimulation

Let's talk stimulants.

For most writers throughout the centuries, the preferred item has been the coffee bean, the seed of the genus coffee. Nothing like a good cup of joe in the morning to get the mind rolling, the fingers pounding and the mind coming up with stuff to happen in the scene you're working on.

Of course you can overdo this. Consider the jamoke intake of Honoré de Balzac. He believed coffee's properties were magical, and proved his devotion by writing over one hundred novels, novellas and stories on what was, essentially, speed.

His practice was to wake up around midnight and have his servants cook up the thickest coffee imaginable. Think tar with a little sugar. He'd down brew after brew, for up to fifteen hours, letting the stimulant feed his imagination.

He died of caffeine poisoning at the age of fifty-one.

In more moderate quantities, however, coffee has proved to be universal in its appeal since its discovery in the fifteenth century. According to the definitive treatise All About Coffee (William H. Ukers, 1922):

> All nations do it homage. It has become recognized as a human necessity. It is no longer a luxury or an indulgence; it is a corollary of human energy and human efficiency. People love coffee because of its two-fold effect—the pleasurable sensation and the increased efficiency it produces.
>
> Coffee has an important place in the rational diet of all the civilized peoples of earth. It is a democratic beverage. Not only is it the drink of fashionable society, but it is also a favorite beverage of the men and women who do the world's work, whether they toil with brain or brawn. It has been acclaimed "the most grateful lubricant known to the human machine," and "the most delightful taste in all nature."

Science is also demonstrating coffee's benefits:

> Doctors found that between three and five cups of coffee a day would be the optimum amount for an individual to consume to prevent the development of a neurodegenerative illness.
>
> In scientific terms, it is believed this is due to the presence high levels of compounds known as polyphenols in coffee having a protective effect on the brain. Previous studies have shown the beverage can reduce a person's risk of developing Alzheimer's by as much as 20 percent.

Now, if you don't like coffee, try tea. My two favorites are Morning Thunder and Roastaroma, both from Celestial Seasonings.

Put your hot liquid into a cup with the word WRITER on it.

Then write.

Stimulants to avoid

Through the years writers have tried many other forms of stimulation, some of which have proved destructive. Like drugs. While LSD may have led to mind-altering visions for William Burroughs and Ken Kesey, it destroyed their writing, productivity and careers.

We all know this now: Don't do drugs.

There are other things to avoid.

Excessive Alcohol

The literary landscape is covered with sad tales of writers who abused the bottle. Some used to reduce the stress of a writer's life. Others thought they actually wrote better with booze in their system. It's a fool's bet.

Don't make like a Faulkner or a Hemingway or a Fitzgerald or a Kerouac. All of them lost their battle with hooch to one degree or another.

On the other hand, John D. MacDonald treated his writing like a day job. At five p.m. he knocked off and had a martini. He did not let that lead to problem drinking.

"One martini is all right," wrote author James Thurber. "Two are too many, and three are not enough."

Energy Drinks

Between 2007 and 2011, emergency room visits involving energy drinks doubled to more than 20,000, according to a report from the Substance Abuse and Mental Health Services Administration.

From U.S. News & World Report:

> While experts believe it's safe for most healthy adults to consume up to 400 milligrams of caffeine a day – about the equivalent of one venti 20-ounce Starbucks coffee or two shots of 5-Hour Energy, CSPI reports – downing multiple energy drinks daily could quickly put someone over that limit, increasing their risk for headaches as well as boost blood pressure and heart rate.
>
> Some groups, including children and adolescents, pregnant and breastfeeding women, and people with heart conditions, are advised to avoid them altogether. Athletes, too, might be at higher risk for complications if they guzzle energy drinks before a race or game. One 2014 study in the British Journal of Nutrition, for example, found that while energy drinks improved athletes' performance, they were more likely to experience insomnia, nervousness and stimulation hours after the competition.

Food Abuse

There are foods that help creativity, and foods that hinder it. For example, foods that are processed, have loads of artificial ingredients, that are based in trans fat—these have long-term negative effects on the brain.

Intake of too much sugar or sodium can lead to a spike-and-crash syndrome that makes you feel like a lump of lard and puts your brain to sleep.

Which does not mean you can't *ever* indulge yourself. Personally, I need an L.A. street dog every six months or so. That's a bacon-wrapped hot dog, grilled, placed on a bun and topped with sautéed onions and bell peppers, some tomato and cilantro *al fresco salsa*—and, if I'm feeling frisky, a couple of grilled jalapeños on top.

This is not my everyday fare.

I suggest you don't make it yours.

What should you eat? I'm not going to play nutritionist here. You can do your own research and find your own preferences. I will say that I like to have protein in the morning. During the day I try to eat good fiber and wash it out with water. I like fish, especially salmon and tuna, and fruit and nuts.

My motto is, don't eat stupidly.

There's my diet book: *The Don't Be Stupid When You Eat Diet.*

Perseverance

"The two most valued attributes in the writer's character are faith in self and dogged persistence."
- Leonard Bishop

Rejection sucks.

It comes in a variety of forms, too. There's a never-ending supply of rejection available to all writers, and it's usually ladled out from a great, big bucket to a long line of scribes standing in the rain.

All writers have suffered the flames of rejection. (Okay, there may be a small handful of exceptions, but they prove the rule, don't they?)

The thing is, what do you do about it?

First, you decide you're never going to quit.

L. Sprague de Camp was a writer from the Golden Age of Science Fiction, the America of the 1930s, and continued writing until his death in 2000 at the age of 92. He was the author of over 120 Science Fiction and Fantasy novels and several hundred short stories. The kind of writer I admire, one who worked hard at his craft and kept producing pages. Why? Because if he didn't, he didn't eat.

He once wrote, "One needs natural talent, much physical energy (which calls for a strict regimen of diet and exercise), and the resilience to bounce back after the most shattering disappointment and frustration."

Talent? You need some, but it is the least important of the attributes for writerly success. It's taking the talent you have to the highest level you can that counts.

1. Develop rhino skin

You have to have a thick hide to make it in this game. Rejection, failure, negative reviews, snide comments on social media or around the Thanksgiving table - these all hurt. The trick is not to let these things damage you. Handle them like a good rhino handles tsetse flies.

Use writer self-talk. When you get pummeled, say to yourself, *I can take it, just like all the great writers of the past had to.*

Resist the urge to self-talk this way: *Where did I put the gin?*

2. Do the sixty-minute comeback

Remember the movie *Analyze This?* Billy Crystal plays a psychiatrist helping mob boss Robert De Niro with a variety of mental health issues. At one point he urges an out of control De Niro to hit a pillow. De Niro pulls out a gun and shoots several rounds into the innocent furniture.

Billy sarcastically asks do you feel better? And in all sincerity De Niro answers, yeah, I do.

This is what all writers should do. Let me amend that statement. Don't use a gun. Feel free to use a pillow and sock it with your fist at the point when you are feeling terrible about some form of rejection or disappointment.

Take thirty minutes to completely feel what you're feeling. Shout, talk to yourself, cry if you must, splash water on your face, eat a large bowl of ice cream. Whatever it is, let yourself feel of feelings for sixty minutes, but no more.

Set a timer for this.

When the timer beeps, set it for another thirty minutes. During this thirty minutes, you *write*. I mean it. Write! Write *anything*.

You can write the next scene of your WIP.

You can write in your journal.

You can write something random.

You can write a letter to your future self.

You can start an entirely new story or novel, not knowing what it will be.

Whatever it is, give yourself fully to it. Write. Don't stop, except to take a few breaths or refill the coffee.

After sixty minutes of writing something interesting will happen. The rejection might still hurt, but it won't be as bad. I guarantee you it won't.

And if later on it comes back to try to bite you, head it off with another writing stint. Five, ten, thirty minutes.

Writing, you see, is your best medicine.

Always.

"Don't quit," says writer Andre Dubus. "It's very easy to quit during the first ten years."

Expectations

The world's great religious and philosophical thinkers have pretty much reached a consensus when it comes to the matter of how to make yourself miserable.

You set up expectations.

Then, when they don't happen, you're unhappy.

So what should you do?

Buddha said, Get rid of all desire.

Epictetus said, Stop thinking about things you can't control. "He who desires … the things which are not in his power can neither be faithful nor free, but must change with them and be tossed about by them as in a tempest."

Here's the thing about expectations. When you don't have them, and receive some good thing, you are pleasantly surprised, and can thus enjoy the outcome. If it does not come about, you don't get knocked down about it because you weren't setting yourself up to expect it.

But if you set up big expectations (or strong desires) and don't get the thing, it can ruin your day, your week, and if you don't watch out, your life.

Now, it's tough to manage expectations and strong desires. We are human.

But as the sages have taught us down through the ages, our greatest challenge is to learn how to manage our humanity.

It's not a skill a lot of people master.

As writers, we have desires for our writing. We set goals. We dream dreams.

What we have to do is have a good, long talk with ourselves and learn to tamp down the expectation factor.

Let's say you're about to release a book. Maybe through a publishing house, maybe on your own.

Your mind starts to form pictures. Maybe it's a picture of the New York Times Bestseller list. You see it, you see the titles and authors, and you imagine your title and your name being there. Maybe you're modest about it and you see your book listed at #5.

That picture becomes a recurring image. Your brain embeds it like a GIF on your visual cortex, so it plays over and over.

To manage the expectation, you have to delete the image.

The good news is, you are in control of your thoughts.

The science of Neuro-Linguistic Programming offers practices for managing those thoughts, primarily through visualization. The big insight in NLP is that our thoughts have mental pictures associated with them, and those pictures control our *feelings.*

Most of the time we don't focus on the image, or do anything conscious with it. We just feel: happy, sad, depressed, hopeful.

Yes, there is sometimes a chemical component to negative feelings, particularly depression. That's something that needs real treatment.

But most of the time we *can* gain a measure of control over our feelings by manipulating the pictures in our mind.

Next time you get some disappointing news, observe your feelings. Notice how you feel, then immediately locate the image of it in your mind. That picture might turn out to be the face of the agent who sent you the rejection. You can see him sitting in his office (you don't have to know what his office actually looks like; you are letting the picture in your mind have its own way).

Whatever the picture is, dwell on it. Make it clear.

Now, create a new picture in your mind, a positive one, one that shows you acting in a successful way.

For example, you see yourself typing away on a new novel.

Or bursting with creativity as you write down ideas.

Or you, studying the craft of writing, highlighting a book.

All of these are things that are within your power to control.

Now do the following:

1. Let the negative image come to you in full, living color.

2. See it, feel it.

3. Now, freeze the image and remove the color, making it black and white.

4. Next, make the image opaque so it's barely visible, a dull gray.

5. Now, in full-color, let your positive image *explode* through the gray, as if the gray were made of tissue paper that vanishes into a thousand bits. Dwell on the new image until you *feel* positive.

Repeat these steps as necessary to get rid of the negative pictures.

From time to time you might find the original negative, the image you want to get rid of, trying to force its way back in. When that happens, repeat steps 3 - 5. You will find you can do that quickly and easily.

The result is that the negative image will recur less and less frequently, and also be weaker in its effects.

So go ahead and let dreams motivate you to set goals. But don't let your dreams become *expectations.* Always concentrate on what is within your power: your ability to sit down at your keyboard and write, to study the craft, to *work.*

Self-Possession

Deep down in every writer, to a greater or lesser degree, is the desire to be recognized and admired by their peers. It's understandable, it's human, and it is an acid drip of negativity that will burn a hole in your writer's soul if you don't get rid of it.

When you put your emotional well being into the hands of a group, you are at the mercy of forces over which you have absolutely no control. Your happiness depends upon other people's reactions, and on some accomplishment you believe should lead to positive vibes from said group.

It's a losing game.

For one thing, you can never tell if writing a certain book will achieve the results you desire. For another, you have no way to influence what others will think about that book—outside of the book itself.

The third factor is that the approval you desire almost never rises to the level that you want it to. There is always another writer who gets greater admiration and acclaim. You end up like a dog waiting for scraps to fall from that table.

That's no way to live.

The need for acceptance and approval and validation is a formula for constant disappointment and the temptation to take to drink.

A long time ago, when I was first living in New York trying to become an actor, I suffered greatly from this need for approval. It haunted me. I kept chasing it. It was always out of my reach.

Then one day I got a piece of advice from someone which has stayed with me ever since. This person told me: *What other people think of you is none of your business.*

It was one of the most important life lessons I ever learned. I have no control over what other people think of me. What I do have control over are my values, my goals, and my attempts to live up to them.

The only people whose opinions I care about are those who are close to me, who I love, who love me, and who I want to honor with my behavior.

When I make a boneheaded mistake and my wife gently points it out, I will listen. If I disappoint a friend, I will apologize and try to make amends.

If I hurt a stranger by mistake, of course I'll be sorry, and say so. That's just being civil.

But outside of those instances, I can't be concerned with what other people think of me.

I also know that many thoughts people hold are irrational, sometimes hateful, sometimes envious, and I'm not going to spend my life trying to sort that all out.

So what do you do about this creeping need for approval?

Two things.

First, say to yourself, over and over, until it is ingrained in your brain: "What other people think of me and my writing is none of my business. I don't need other people's approval to be a writer!"

Second, practice generosity. Give to the writing community. Encourage other writers. Be a positive force.

Almost every year I go to a convention called Bouchercon. It's an annual gathering of writers and fans, mostly who enjoy mysteries, thrillers, and crime novels.

At all of the 'Cons I've gone to, I've had the chance to talk to Lee Child. He is, of course, one of the most successful authors in the world, and he always has time to talk to fellow writers without pretension and without airs.

I respect that.

Make generosity your goal, rather than seeking some kind of amorphous validation in order to be happy in your writing.

Envy

A sound heart is the life of the flesh:
But envy the rottenness of the bones. - Proverbs 14:30

Envy is a monster, a green-eyed one, and all writers seem to fall prey to it from time to time. It sneaks up on you. Your day can be going along quite nicely, you've written a great scene, you see someone has left a positive review … and then you see what some other writer has done and bam, all of a sudden this envy thing grabs the back of your neck.

For some writers, envy is debilitating. If it's not dealt with it can be like a food poisoning: something I wouldn't wish on anyone, with some very few exceptions.

Anne Lamott has a hilarious chapter on envy in her book *Bird by Bird:*

> If you continue to write, you are probably going to have to deal with [envy] because some wonderful, dazzling successes are going to happen for some of the most awful, angry, undeserving writers you know—people who are, in other words, not you … You are going to feel awful beyond words. You are going to have a number of

> days in a row where you hate everyone and don't believe in anything. If you do know the author whose turn it is, he or she will inevitably say that it will be your turn next, which is what the bride always says to you at each successive wedding, while you grow older and more decayed.
>
> It can wreak just the tiniest bit of havoc with your self-esteem to find that you are hoping for small bad things to happen to this friend—for, say, her head to blow up.

Let's dig a little deeper into envy.

Here's a surprise for you: Envy is 5% positive. That's the 5% that tells you that you care deeply about what you're doing, that you want it to matter to other people, the way some other writers matter.

The other 95% is toxic. Fifty-seven percent of you wishes something bad would happen to the object of your envy (see Ann's passage, above).

The other 38% of envy is you feeling bad about yourself and your writing, thinking you're no good and you don't have what it takes, and maybe never will.

(By the way, those percentages are from my own unscientific imagination, so don't envy my methodology).

So you have to deal with envy, and the best time to do that is before it hits you.

The first step in dealing with writer envy is to recognize it when it happens, and analyze it the way I've described. Acknowledge that it has one, and only one, good sign: it shows you care about your writing.

Now turn that into positive energy.

Instead of dwelling on the person you envy, write something about the feeling and yourself. Journal about it. Confess to yourself in person. Pour out your soul. Open a vein.

Next, tell yourself not to hold anything against the other writer. The other writer is just doing his thing and getting his own reward.

But what if he's a rotten human being? What if he's like Mozart and you're like Salieri?

Then go ahead and wish that his head would explode.

For five minutes.

Then move on.

Create a credo for yourself. A credo is a statement of purpose, a vision statement of sorts. Jack London, for example, had a famous credo which moved him to become one of the most prolific authors of his day:

> I would rather be ashes than dust!
> I would rather that my spark should burn out in a brilliant blaze than it should be stifled by dry-rot.
> I would rather be a superb meteor, every atom of me in magnificent glow, than a sleepy and permanent planet.
> The function of man is to live, not to exist.
> I shall not waste my days trying to prolong them.
> I shall use my time.

A healthy writer's ego sounds something like this: *I write because I believe I have what it takes to tell stories. I write because an inner fire compels me, and I am committed to working hard to make myself the best writer I can be. I write for readers. They are my ultimate validation, and what any other writer writes does not affect that at all. I am a writer, and will write and never stop.*

Who are you, writer? Who do you want to be?

Write it down, then be that writer.

Forget about the other person's success and go about creating your own.

Speed

You want to write faster?

There are ways.

Chugging Red Bull is not one of them. Try these instead.

Permission

Repeat after me: *Don't get it right. Just get it written.*

That's your first draft mantra.

See if you can up your writing quota by 10% just by listening to yourself say, *Don't get it right. Just get it written.*

Practice

Turn off your inner editor. This is the voice that's talking to you as you write. It's judging you. It's saying that you can't do this or that because it violates some "rule." It tells you to stop writing because it's just not "working." On bad days, when the inner editor is very grumpy, it will plain tell you that you suck.

You can practice shutting off that voice by writing in sprints.

Determine to write for five minutes without stopping.
Set a timer.
Use a writing prompt (you can find these online).
Write, and don't stop.
You'll become a faster writer this way, naturally.

Write first thing

Getting some writing out of the way early will increase your speed later in the day. Sort of like a major league ballplayer who swings a weighted bat before going to the plate.

"But I'm just not a morning person!"

Oh really? You're a person, right? And you get up in the morning, yes? And you find a way to get some coffee and hop on Facebook, don't you?

I don't want to hear that morning person jazz anymore. DO NOT OPEN ANY SOCIAL MEDIA, INTERNET BROWSER, OR EMAIL until you have written 250 words.

"But I'm so foggy, I just can't think ..."

Good! Don't think at all. Just write, and write fast. The discipline of getting down 250 words without delay will train your brain to be up and at 'em throughout the day.

Do not edit, spell check, correct, or otherwise stop your flow until the 250 is done. (Here's a little secret. When you get to 250 you're going to want to keep going. So go!)

You can also help your writing brain along by doing this:

Leave off your day's writing mid-scene

This lets your subconscious cook during the night, and when you sit down to work on your WIP you'll be back in the flow immediately. Hemingway even used to stop mid-sentence. I can imagine him writing:

He saw the fish and the fish was good. It was a good fish. It was a fish like the good bull in Spain that summer with Stein. Yes, and the beer was warm that summer, but it was good beer, it was

How easily he could continue the next day: *beer that was brave and true and good.*

Take 60 seconds to map out a scene

To write any scene in a work of fiction, you need to know at least three things:

1. What does the viewpoint character want? This is the *objective.*

2. What's going to stand in his way? These are the *obstacles.* They can come in the form of other characters who oppose him, physical circumstances, inner turmoil. But without obstacles there is no conflict to the scene. No conflict = dull.

3. What will be the *outcome?* Will it be positive (objective realized) or negative (objective frustrated)? If the former, ask how it can lead to further trouble. If the latter, how can it make the situation worse?

And as a bonus question, ask: what surprising thing can happen in this scene? Anything that the reader would not anticipate.

Now you don't have to go hunting for what your scene is about.

Write it, and write it fast.

Learn to dictate

Writing now includes speaking–via voice recognition apps. Some sophisticated programs can be had for a price. But native programs, like Google Docs, are functional and getting better.

Dictation is faster than flying fingers but it's not perfect. You'll need to edit carefully. And be aware that you'll probably have a different "voice" when you dictate (referring to style). Many writers first draft via dictation, then layer in style when they edit.

Personally, I prefer typing, but will use dictation on occasion, like when I have my phone and earbuds and am not at my computer.

A quick page is a quick page. It all adds up, which is the point!

When you edit, that's when to go slow

If you're worried about sacrificing quality when you write fast, your remedy is to edit slow. You'll learn your optimum speed when measured against your own standards for your writing.

Some writers, like Isaac Asimov, develop a stripped down and utilitarian style in order to write faster. Tell the story clearly using simple language.

Others, like John D. MacDonald (who was quite prolific) seek a certain amount of "unobtrusive poetry" in their style. They will spend more time on actual sentences, usually when polishing a final draft.

What style you desire is, of course, up to you. So match your speed to your goals and write accordingly.

Comparison

Comparison is death to a writer. Don't look up or down. Look at the page in front of you and nail it! - James Scott Bell

Every day I can look at another writer's career or recent success and get bent. Or I can be grateful for the career I have and keep doing what I do, which is write and try to do it better every time out.

There's something tremendously satisfying about the latter. I refuse to compare myself to others. Twenty years ago, unpublished, if I'd been shown my present career in a crystal ball I would have said *Yes! Let me have that!*

The phenomenal tennis player Andy Roddick had the misfortune to come up at the same time as guy named Roger Federer, one of the greatest players of all time. Roddick's record against Federer was 2 wins, 20 losses.

Late in his career Roddick remarked, "You keep moving forward until you decide to stop. At this point I've not decided to stop, so I'll keep moving forward."

You can't let comparisons with another writer's career stop you from moving forward.

There is only one Lee Child, Stephen King, Janet Evanovich, J. K. Rowling.

They have succeeded because they are good, and also because the Wheel of Fortune selected them to go to the stratosphere.

You cannot control the Wheel of Fortune.

All you can do is write books *good enough* to get a spot on the Wheel. And if it doesn't hit the big prize like it does for another writer, you get on with your primary task: writing the best book you can.

But what about competition? Isn't writing, like other things in life, about competing with other authors?

Writing is not a zero-sum game. Someone else does not have to lose in order for you to win. And winning itself is a slippery concept in the arts.

The only worthwhile competition is with yourself.

Sure, you can look at another writer and seek to emulate what that writer does well. Not *copy*. Emulate.

If you like a writer's style, study what he does and then create your own style.

If you like an author's twisty plots, study them out and twist up your own.

If you admire an author's production, seek to up your own word count.

Measure your success by what you do with measurable goals. That's where competitive *fire* comes in. That's what the great champions have.

Fire up yourself.

Look at your discipline, and if you've fallen short get mad at yourself for about thirty seconds, give yourself a pep talk, and make plans to do better.

I always try to do this just after Christmas. I look back at my writing year and assess my performance.

In fact, as I write this, it's Christmas Day and I see I've

fallen a little short of my word count goal for the year. I also feel I was a little "soft" about things. What I mean is that while, by most measures, things have never been better in my writing life, I feel as though this past year I sort of "coasted."

I'm always the first one up at my house, so I got some coffee and flicked on the tube and started watching an ESPN documentary called "I Hate Christian Laettner." It's about the famous Duke basketball player who engendered such hot feelings from fans and other schools.

But where all the hatred might have wilted another player, it fired Laettner up. He just went out on the floor and beat you. All with an attitude of swagger and subtle humor.

So I'm making it a goal to up my fire in my own writing.

How?

By making sure I'm excited about writing. See my chapter on Inspiration.

Also by giving myself more pep talks when I don't reach a word count goal.

And by having what basketball coach Rick Pitino calls the PHD attitude: poor, hungry, driven.

But also to remember something equally important: rest. You have to balance drive and rest, action and relaxation. That is the subject of our next chapter.

Fight

Marcus Aurelius, the stoic emperor of Rome, and a pretty good writer, said life is more a wrestling match than it is a dance.

Which means sometimes you just have to fight.

We've talked about perseverance, and about coming back.

Now I want to talk about fighting, which offers its own rewards.

I don't mean fighting with other people. We have enough of that, and it sucks. Literally. It sucks joy out of you, and always you should write with joy.

I mean fighting the good fight. Having the attitude that you are ready to make the very best of every waking moment.

A former president said this:

> It is not the critic who counts; not the man who points out how the strong man stumbles, or where the doer of deeds could have done them better. The credit belongs to the man who is actually in the arena, whose face is marred by dust and

> sweat and blood; who strives valiantly; who errs, who comes short again and again, because there is no effort without error ... but who does actually strive to do the deeds; who knows great enthusiasms, the great devotions; who spends himself in a worthy cause; who at the best knows in the end the triumph of high achievement, and who at the worst, if he fails, at least fails while daring greatly, so that his place shall never be with those cold and timid souls who neither know victory nor defeat. - Theodore Roosevelt

Keep punching, the old boxing trainers used to say, because that always gives you a puncher's chance.

If you don't throw a punch, you'll never land one.

"You miss one hundred percent of the shots you never take," said the great hockey player Wayne Gretzky.

It's not whether you get knocked down that counts. It's whether you get back up.

For a writer, the punches are paragraphs. The jabs are sentences. A new scene is another round.

And you will never be counted out so long as you're ready to answer the bell, every day you write.

Can you tell I like boxing metaphors?

Jake LaMotta, the middleweight boxer who was the subject of the Martin Scorsese/Robert De Niro film *Raging Bull*, was a legend of resiliency. He'd never stop coming at you, and he simply would not go down.

No matter what punishment was rained upon him (most savagely by Sugar Ray Robinson), Jake LaMotta refused to be knocked out.

You have a keyboard. No one can ever make you stop using it.

Stress

Some time ago the astute Kristine Kathryn Rusch wrote an amusing post about how her mind felt with all the freedom that comes from being an indie writer ("Attack of the Popcorn Kittens!!!!", Kriswrites.com, July 24, 2013). The post was accompanied by the YouTube vid "Kittens Gone Wild." Little kitties in a shared pen jumping all over the place in random fashion.

That is what an indie writer's mind can often feel like. So much freedom! So many things to write! And yet so many marketing hats to put on, and a ton of petty tasks that seem to repeat, over and over again.

Lest ye think this is just an indie conundrum, it's also increasingly a picture of a tradpub author's brain, because so much of the marketing onus now falls upon the writer. Publishers are insisting upon "platform" before they offer contracts. When a book is released the harried in-house publicity person has little time for any single author. So you better be out there doing a hundred different things...every day!

If you don't watch out the resulting stress might grab your

good endorphins and slam them to the mat like an amped-up Conor McGregor (which is redundant).

Enough of that and you could end up tired or with a chronic case of the blues.

Here's how a typical popcorn kitten scenario might play out.

> You're writing your WIP, an essential scene where your protagonist has to apply for a new job. In your pre-planning you decided that job would be as a hairdresser. Or, since you are a notorious pantser, you came up with that on the spot.
>
> You don't know all that much about the hairdressing business. If you are a wise writer, you put a mark in your manuscript that will tell you to do the research later. Then you'll write as much of the scene as you can, based on what you know about human nature and job interviews—and if you don't know about either of these, you should quit writing and join the Navy. Then get out and write a novel about the Navy.
>
> Instead, you decide to leave your WIP and jump on the internet for some "quick" research. As you look at search results, you see a book called *What Every Writer Needs To Know About Writing Hairdresser Interview Scenes*, and you click over to Amazon to check it out. Seems reasonable at $2.99, but just to make sure you don't spend your discretionary Starbucks money like a fool, you download the free sample.
>
> But while you are on Amazon you see a recommendation for a mystery series about hairdressers. You know the author. She's someone you met at Bouchercon. You hop over to the book page

and see 125 five-star reviews and a rank of 1,286 in the paid Kindle store. At a price of $4.99. What? Your self-published stand-alone mystery is only $2.99 and it's ranked 423,679.

You wonder what this other author has that you don't. So you look at her Amazon author page and check out her covers. Wow. Great! Your cover was done by your cousin Axel, a budding commercial artist who lives with his poet girlfriend, Moonglow. Well, you admit, you got what you paid for.

You do a little more research and find out who did this author's covers. You check out the artist's portfolio online and what he is charging. Whoa! That's a healthy chunk!

So you do a little research on how to judge the worth of a book cover. There are many blog posts on this, and you read a few of them. Something else catches your eye on the last one. It's about the importance of book description copy in selling a book. You recall that when you did yours you had a nagging suspicion it was rather plain vanilla, but you were anxious to get the book out because everyone in your critique group was making money self-publishing and you didn't want to be the chump standing on the dock as the ship took off for the Bahamas with all your friends.

You go back to Amazon and find a book called *Book Description Copy for Former Chumps Like Yourself,* and you download that sample. You read that sample, and from the Table of Contents figure out some of what your own description was missing, so you open up a new doc and start writing afresh.

Ten minutes into that a thought pops into

> your head. You don't want to have your protagonist apply for a hairdresser job. No! She should be an insurance investigator!
>
> So you hop back on Google looking for "How to become an insurance investigator." Lo and behold, there's a book called *Insurance Investigation for Former Chumps Like Yourself*. The author has a website. You go to the website and see he has a blog. Gold!
>
> Which reminds you, you were going to try to do some guest posts for various blogs when your book came out. That's publicity! Where was that list again? You search for it ... you need to send out some emails!
>
> You look at the clock. Uh-oh, it's almost time to pick up Lydia from school, and what have you done on your WIP? Fifty-seven words! The last word you typed was *hairdresser*...

I'm sure you can relate. Just as a Molinist theologian can contemplate an infinite number of contingent realities, so you, the writer, have an infinite number of ways you can get distracted, going off in different directions based upon a single pop of a cerebral synapse, one little soft-pawed frolic of a popcorn kitten.

So what's the cure?

Here is one simple trick that can change your life. All it requires is some paper and a little mental discipline.

I call it Nab, Stab and Tab.

First step is to *nab* that thought. Recognize it for what it is—a siren's song to leave what you're focused on and slide into Alice's rabbit hole. You might even say it out loud. "My crazy mind wants me to go on Google right now!"

Next step, *stab*. You want to nail the thought to your desk so it doesn't hop around in your head. You do this by *writing it down*. That's all. I have scratch paper nearby for just this purpose. So in the scenario above, if I suddenly remembered I want to explore guest blogging, I'd write *guest blogging* on the paper.

Then I *immediately* forget about it and get back on task! This is the key moment, the *forgetting*. Get back to work on your WIP!

Finally, when I come up for air and have some time, I'll give each thought a *tab*—I assign it a level of importance, using the A, B, C method (which I detail in my monograph, *How to Manage the Time of Your Life*, available for Kindle.)

A is for highly important, must-do.

B is for what I'd like to do.

C is for items that can wait.

If there is more than one A item, I prioritize these with A1, A2. Same with any Bs and Cs.

Next, I estimate how much time each task will take. I use quarter hour increments. So a task might take me .25 hour or .5 or a full 1 or 2. Whatever.

Finally, I put the A tasks into my weekly schedule in priority order. If there's enough time, I'll put in the Bs. The Cs I usually put off.

This may sound complicated, but it takes only a few seconds to nab and stab. And only a few minutes to tab and schedule.

Yet the benefits are profound. Less stress, more focus on your primary work.

The kittens will start to purr, and then they'll go to sleep.

And you'll sleep better, too.

Burnout

Not even God created for seven days in a row.

Burnout is when the tank is empty and we still have our foot on the pedal. We're stuck and it feels like miles before the next gas station.

With burnout, we feel emotionally—and very often physically—exhausted.

It messes with our heads. We feel we're not good enough. We want to keep going, but can't.

Nor is it something we can "work through." There just isn't the energy.

Instead, we probably feel like chucking the whole thing.

Some of the signs of burnout are:

1. Complete lack of enjoyment. You don't feel any joy in your writing. Instead you think your pen name should be Sisyphus.

2. Pessimism. You tell yourself all this work is not worth it, that you'll never make it. The game is rigged, it's all a matter of luck—and your prospects of getting lucky are just pie-in-the-sky. You feel like a joke.

3. Isolation. In extreme burnout cases, you will think you're alone, a failure, and you don't want people to see you. Nor do you want to see others, especially those who are enjoying some success.

4. Jerkness. If you're not careful, you can become a jerk. In that case, #3 takes care of itself, because no one wants to be around you, either.

The thing to do about burnout is head it off at the pass. And the best way I know is to observe a Writing Sabbath. Just like when God knocked off for the week.

It can be on any day you choose. As I mention in the Discipline chapter, I choose Sunday.

On that day I do not do any writing or even thinking about writing (at least I try not to think about it. It's the day when the Boys in the Basement get to work out in earnest).

It's a good day to catch up on my reading.

And my relationship with my wife! We'll take a trip to the beach, or go up in the hills and look at the view. We'll watch a movie together, have a nice dinner….

If it's football season, I'll watch a game or two.

I try to get out in the sunshine.

What all this means is that the pressure is off.

Though sometimes my mind and my fingers want to write something. It's sort of like the thoroughbred that is primed to run every day, but one day is just hanging out with a blanket and some hay. The legs tremble. The nose sniffs the air.

At times like that I keep my legs calm and my nose in a book.

What about during your writing week?

Two things if you can manage them: get exercise and get very quiet.

The benefits of even short bursts of exercise are well known. Walk around as much as you can, if that's the least you can do.

Follow the Pomodoro Method. Write for twenty-five minutes, then take a five-minute break. Do some walking or deep breathing (with your eyes closed).

Also, I'm a big believer in the power nap. That's a twenty-minute or so stretch of nodding off sometime during the work day. We all have a "zombie time." For me it's around 1 or 2 o'clock. My mind turns to jelly.

So I trained myself to get to sleep quickly and wake up twenty minutes later. You can do this, too. It will take you about two months to instill the habit, if you so desire.

I can sleep almost anywhere. Usually I'll put on some nice rainfall sound, put my feet up on my desk, and lean back with a pair of plastic eye protectors (you know, for the beach or tanning booth) on my face.

Or I'll hit the sofa or bed.

What I find is that my power nap buys me an extra hour or so in the evening.

There is even something called a "caffeine nap." I've started doing that, too. I found that after an early start (when it's nice and dark and quiet in the house), and getting some good writing done and downing a couple cups of joe—if I hit the sack for half an hour, I wake up feeling extra alert and energized.

Lo and behold, there's some research to back that up.

> Coffee clears the body of a chemical called adenosine. Levels of this compound rise while you're awake; when enough accumulates, it helps tell your brain to go to sleep. The chemical is then

broken down while you sleep. Coffee reduces adenosine in the brain, a process that takes about 20 minutes, so coffee followed by a 15-minute nap may maximize alertness. In one study, researchers put sleep-deprived test subjects in driving simulators and found that "caffeine naps" more effectively improved driving performance than cold air, a short break, a nap with no caffeine, or caffeine with no nap. ("What Should You Do After Drinking Coffee?" by Emily Tamkin, *Slate*, Aug. 22, 2014).

Contentment

To fight does not mean you are discontent.

Discontent is a gremlin.

Gremlins are the furry, clawed, sharp-toothed creatures made up by airplane pilots during World War II. When things went wrong with an engine or a wing or a landing gear, it was said that a gremlin got to it. (The greatest story about gremlins is Richard Matheson's "Nightmare at 20,000 Feet," turned into a famous *Twilight Zone* episode starring William Shatner.)

Likewise, in the soul of the writer—or most people striving for achievement—the gremlin of discontent bares his fangs and gets to his dirty work.

Reasons for this are many. We've covered expectations and envy.

As Dennis Prager, an expert on happiness, says, "The Missing Tile Syndrome is a very big obstacle to happiness. So big, in fact, that it makes happiness almost impossible. There will always be something missing in your life. When you see other people's kids, you'll think you see tiles that are missing in your own children. 'Gee, why can't my kids study as hard, or be as polite, or be as bright, or be as good looking, or be as athletic.' The same holds true regarding our spouses, our work, our looks. The list is endless."

Don't make what you *don't have* more important than what you *do* have.

The antidote to discontent is gratitude. Indeed, the sages of all world religions and the sandal-wearing philosophers of Greece and Rome, all recognize that gratitude is essential to one's happiness in life.

So learn to be grateful for what you've got. Start by making a list of all the things you are thankful for. Put down even the smallest things, such as: the ability to think, the power of imagination, the ability to type, friends, family, dogs, cats, sunset, someone close to you who is especially supportive.

You can even learn to be thankful for disasters that have not happened to you. You are not in the tsunami. In line be thankful that you can think and have the ability to take control of your own writing. You can study, you can write more, you can go to a conference, you don't have to take no for an answer, all of these things are worth being thankful for.

One other thought: learn how to withdraw into some solitude daily, and quiet the mind. Let me tell you, it's not easy, especially as we've been trained to have our phones with us every waking moment.

But if you can truly learn the discipline of silence it increases your contentment like nothing else.

The Christian mystic A. W. Tozer counseled:

> Retire from the world each day to some private spot, even if it be only the bedroom (for a while I retreated to the furnace room for want of a better place). Stay in the secret place till the surrounding noises begin to fade out of your heart and a sense of God's presence envelops you.

> Listen for the inward Voice till you learn to recognize it. Stop trying to compete with others…Reduce your interests to a few. Don't try to know what will be of no service to you. Avoid the digest type of mind—short bits of unrelated facts, cute stories and bright sayings….Practice candor, childlike honesty, humility….Practice spiritual concentration.

You have a daily writing time. Find at least fifteen minutes a day when you get quiet. Mute your phone. Breathe.

Power

There is nothing quite like the feeling you get when you do high quality work with high quality efficiency.

Writers who know the craft—and keep growing in it—and who spend the most time on high priority tasks, these are the writers who experience a power vibe.

That, in turn, inspires momentum and action.

It's like a perpetual writing excellence machine.

Below are some power questions. If you'll take the time to go over these carefully it will provide you with a foundation for writing success that will last you a lifetime.

Writing Related

1. What are your strengths as a writer?
2. What aspect of writing brings you the most joy?
3. What kind of books do you love to read?
4. Why are your favorite novels of all time your favorites?
5. What would you tell a potential reader who asks you why he should purchase one of your books?

6. What is your one, primary goal as a writer?
7. What things do you have to do to make that a reality?
8. What obstacles are in your way, and what will you do to overcome them?
9. What are five goals that will serve you in reaching your primary aim?
10. What actions will you take every day toward the achievement of your goals?
11. What are your scores in the 7 Critical Success Factors of Fiction? (Do the worksheet in the chapter on Growth).
12. What craft books to you plan to read over the next year?

Efficiency Related

1. What are your biggest daily distractions?
2. How can you delegate or postpone these items?
3. What is one thing you can eliminate completely from your schedule?
4. Are you setting aside blocks of time for social media and email, and ignoring them during your writing time?
5. Are you giving yourself permission to write faster? (See Speed)
6. Are you getting rest so as to avoid burnout?
7. Are you taking care of your health?

Periodically, perhaps once a year, review these questions and chart your course accordingly. If you do, this will happen:

You will feel the power.

You will love the feeling.

And that's my parting word to you.

Inspiration

Below are some of my favorite quotes on writing. In the past I found that whenever I was in the dumps about writing, reading what other authors have said about it helps. So come browse here whenever you need a boost!

"If you boldly risk writing a novel that might be acclaimed as great, and fail, you could succeed in writing a book that is splendid." – Leonard Bishop

"Work with all your intelligence and love. Work freely and rollickingly as though you were talking to a friend who loves you. Mentally (at least three or four times a day) thumb your nose at all know-it-alls, jeerers, critics, doubters." – Brenda Ueland

"Maintain a pitch next to madness – but never take yourself too seriously." – Tom Robbins

"Self-consciousness is the enemy of all art, be it acting, writing, painting, or living itself, which is the greatest art of all." – Ray Bradbury

"The writer who is a real writer is a rebel who never stops." – William Saroyan

"How vain it is to sit down to write when you have not stood up to live." – Thoreau

"Ray Bradbury told me to put a sign on my typewriter: Don't Think. It works miracles. I suggest a sign above it: Have Fun." – Richard Bach

"I decided early on that I was going to be a writer and that whether I succeeded or failed, I was still going to be a writer." – Joe David Bellamy

"I decided that I would continue to write as long as I lived, even if I never sold one thing, because that was what I wanted out of my life." – George Bernau

"One may achieve remarkable writerly success while flunking all the major criteria for success as a human being. Try not to do that." – Michael Bishop

"Write because you love it, and develop a zen of rejection that includes a healthy disregard for agents and editors." – Gordon De Marco, crime writer

"The chief thing is desire. You've really got to want to do it, you've really got to want to tell that story. And you have to be able to set goals for yourself to get it done." – F. Paul Wilson.

Robert Heinlein's Rules of Writing:

1. You must write.
2. You must finish what you write.

"Give the best part of every day to yourself. Get up early and write if you can. Once you've put words to paper, you've conquered the day. Then you can put bread on the table and beer in the icebox." – Jack Dann

"The trick is not to give up, ever." – Barnaby Conrad.

"Remember, almost no writers had it easy when starting out. If they did, everyone would be a bestselling author. The ones who make it are the stubborn, persistent people who develop a thick skin, defy the rejection, and keep the material out there, trolling." – Barnaby Conrad.

"I tell would-be writers that there are three things to forget about. First, talent. I used to worry that I had no talent, and it compelled me to work harder. Second, inspiration. Habit will serve you a lot better. And third, imagination. Don't worry, you have it." – Octavia Butler

"If you want to write fiction, the best thing you can do is take two aspirins, lie down in a dark room, and wait for the feeling to pass. If it persists, you probably ought to write a novel." – Lawrence Block.

"Envy can be a positive motivator. Let it inspire you to work harder for what you want." – Robert Bringle

"I get both elated and scared when I come to the end of a novel. Elated because it will soon be over; scared because I'm afraid I'll blow it all." – Raymond Obstfeld.

"You must want it enough. Enough to take all the rejections, enough to pay the price of disappointment and discouragement while you are learning. Like any other artist you must learn your craft–then you can add all the genius you like." – Phyllis Whitney

"The reader has certain rights. He bought your story. Think of this as an implicit contract. He's entitled to be entertained, instructed, amused; maybe all three. If he quits in the middle, or puts the book down, feeling his time has been wasted, you're in violation." – Larry Niven

"Always stop the day's work when you know exactly what your next paragraph will be when you start up again the next day." – William Heffernan

"Treat it as a job–not a mystical calling. Then you'll get up every morning and go "to work" instead of waiting for the muse to attend you." – Jean Brody

"Keep working. Keep trying. Keep believing. You still might not make it, but at least you gave it your best shot. If you don't have calluses on your soul, this isn't for you. Take up knitting instead." – David Eddings

"The beautiful part of writing is that you don't have to get it right the first time, unlike, say, a brain surgeon." – Robert Cormier

"First drafts are always lousy." – Richard Reeves

"You fail more than you succeed, even when your efforts get published and you get paid." – Larry Grobel

"Never assume that a rejection of your stuff is also a rejection of you as a person. Unless it's accompanied by a punch in the nose." – Ron Goulart

"Start each writing session by rewriting what was written the day before. That way the writer avoids the agony of starting to write over and over again." – Patrick F. McManus

"The most debilitating thing about writing is that the voice inside us, the voice we trust more than others, says, "You're not good enough, you're not smart enough, what you wrote yesterday really stinks." What aspiring writers should keep in mind is that we all hear that voice, and sometimes that voice lies to us. In fact, when it comes to writing, that voice almost always lies to us. Midway through a book you are going to read back and think, 'This is awful.' Now it may be awful, but it also may be wonderful and you've simply read it so many times your ear has gone deaf. Don't listen to that voice." – Randy Waine White

"Don't give up. I don't think any other advice works. Writing is one of those things where you just have to do it. There will be far more people to discourage you than to encourage you. The time never comes to you, the inspiration doesn't come to you. You just sit down and do it." – James Lee Burke.

"A writer is a vessel for something larger than himself. He was given the gift. He has a charge, and that is to tell his particular vision to the rest of the world. But once a writer believes that somehow he has acquired the gift of his own accord, that he's earned it, that he deserves all the success, the gift will leave him. It'll float away like a helium balloon. I'm convinced of that. Humility is something an artist must have, or he won't endure as an artist. His creative powers will dissipate as soon as he sees himself as an end in himself." – James Lee Burke

"The only book that should ever be written is one that flows up from the heart, forced out by inward pressure." – A.W. Tozer

"The inclination to write is common. Sometimes every other stranger who hears that I write confesses a desire, even a plan, to do the same. It doesn't surprise me that so few of them ever follow through. Consider how much is required. Time on the grand scale: years of patient practice to develop craft. Time on the ordinary scale: a few daily minutes or hours, getting a draft down, rethinking it, polishing. Concentration: the right environment, and freedom from distracting worry. And above all, conviction: the belief that the words on the page matter and the confidence to hang on to that belief in the face of a skeptical world." – Bruce Holland Rogers.

"There is the reward of the storyteller, seated cross-legged in the middle of the bazaar, filling the need of humanity in the humdrum course of an ordinary day for magic and tales of distant wonders, for disguised moralizing which will set everyday transactions into larger perspectives, for the compression of great matters into digestible portions, for the shaping of mysteries into sharply-edged and comprehensible symbols." – Irwin Shaw

"Every hour you spend writing is an hour not spent fretting about your writing." – Dennis Palumbo

"I only write when I'm inspired, and I see to it that I'm inspired at nine o'clock every morning." – Peter De Vries

"When a reader fully believes our story, both intellectually and emotionally, he moves in and unpacks his bags. No longer a tourist living out of a suitcase, ordering room service and watching suspiciously from his hotel window as the natives bustle on the street below, he has become, for the moment at least, a native himself. He changes into comfortable clothes, strolls the avenues, eats in open-air cafes, even tries the local catch-of-the-day. He turns another page in the book. Anything is possible. Who knows? He might even fall in love." – Rebecca McClanahan, Word Painting

"There have been great societies that did not use the wheel, but there have been no societies that did not tell stories." – Ursula K. LeGuin

"In the end, writing is like a prison, an island from which you will never be released but which is a kind of paradise: the solitude, the thoughts, the incredible joy of putting into words the essence of what you for the moment understand and with your whole heart want to believe." – James Salter

"I could claim any number of highflown reasons for writing, just as you can explain certain dog behavior as submission to the alpha, or even a moral choice. But maybe it's that they're dogs, and that's what dogs do." – Amy Hempel

"You're a writer when you're impatient to get back to work. You're a writer when, in the company of others, you're staring off into space, knee-deep in words and sentences, fitting them into the literary puzzle of your emerging piece of work. You're a writer when, given the choice of other occupations, you find you have no choice." – Helen F. Brassel

Resources

Below are some of my writing resources listed by subject. If you would like to be on my mailing list to receive occasional notices about my new books or deals, please go to my website: www.jamesscottbell.com. And keep writing!

Plot & Structure

Write Your Novel From the Middle
Plot & Structure
Super Structure
Conflict & Suspense

Revision

Revision & Self-Editing
27 Fiction Writing Blunders - And How Not to Make Them

Dialogue

How to Write Dazzling Dialogue

Publishing & Career

How to Make a Living as a Writer
The Art of War for Writers
Self-Publishing Attack!

Writing & The Writing Life

Writing Fiction for All You're Worth
Fiction Attack!
How to Achieve Your Goals and Dreams
How to Manage the Time of Your Life

Recommended Writing Blogs

KillZoneblog.com

WriterUnboxed.com

WritersHelpingWriters.net

HelpingWritersBecomeAuthors.com

TheCreativePenn.com

Fiction by James Scott Bell

The Mike Romeo Thrillers

Book 1 - *Romeo's Rules*
Book 2 - *Romeo's Way*

The Trials of Kit Shannon Historical Series

Book 1 - *City of Angels*
Book 2 - *Angels Flight*
Book 3 - *Angel of Mercy*
Book 4 - *A Greater Glory*
Book 5 - *A Higher Justice*
Book 6 - *A Certain Truth*

The Ty Buchanan Legal Thrillers

Book 1 - *Try Dying*
Book 2 - *Try Darkness*
Book 3 - *Try Fear*

Standalone Suspense

Don't Leave Me
Final Witness
Blind Justice
Watch Your Back
One More Lie

About the Author

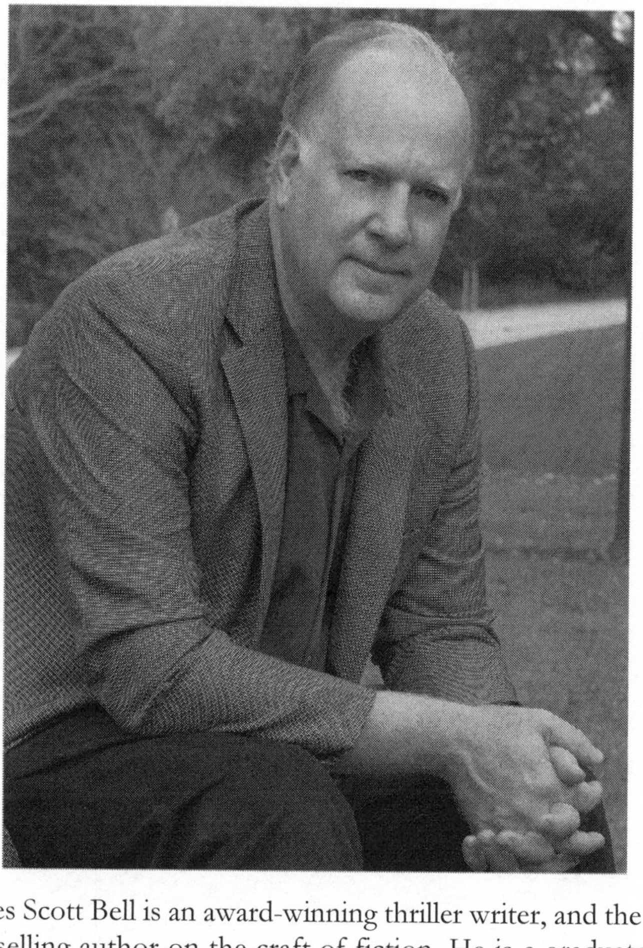

James Scott Bell is an award-winning thriller writer, and the #1 bestselling author on the craft of fiction. He is a graduate of the USC Law School and U.C. Santa Barbara, where he studied writing with Raymond Carver. A finalist for the International Thriller Writers Award, he is third-generation Los Angeles, where most of his books are set. Visit his website www.jamesscottbell.com

44147260R00087

Made in the USA
Middletown, DE
29 May 2017